a *for* Author

CW01663433

Social Media *for* Authors

Book Marketing for Writers Who'd Rather *Write*

Jennifer Lovett Herbranson

Social Media *for* Authors: Marketing for Writers Who'd Rather Write

ISBN (print book) 978-1-7333-961-0-3

ISBN (ebook)978-1-7333-961-1-0

Statistics from Omnicore Agency, Forrester Analytics, Edison Research, Pew Research Center, Audio Publishers Association reprinted with permission.

Quotes from Rand Fishkin, Jeff Bulas, and Joanna Penn reprinted with permission.

Editing by Sandra Wendel, Write On, Inc. and Mark Reid, AuthorPackages.
Proofreading by Jessica Snyder, Jessica Snyder Edits
Cover design by Heidi Sutherlin
Interior design by Heidi Sutherlin

Published by Mustard Couch Press, a subsidiary of TJC Enterprises, LLC, 2308 Mt Vernon Ave #440, Alexandria, VA 22301

Visit www.jenniferlovettherbranson.com

Sign up for Writer Nation news

To Ronald Cree.

He will never know how much he impacted me and supported me simply by being who he was.

And

to all Writers for having the courage to share your stories with the world.

Contents

Introduction 1

1. It's Been Years, but I Still Don't Know Jack 13

Online Marketing: A No-Brainer (Why Authors Need to be Online) 16

Author Platform: You the Author (Develop Your Public Persona) 17

Who Reads This Stuff? (Define Your Reader) 22

Give 'em All the Feels (How to Reach Your Reader) 26

2. This Internet Is Huge 31

Too Many Social Media Platforms (Where Am I Supposed to Post?) 31

Why Aren't People Working in the Afternoon? (When to Post) 50

Easy, for Pete's Sake, Make it Easy (Rule of Thirds) 52

Seriously, Give Me Back My Time! (Social Media Scheduler) 57

3. Yes, My Blooper Reel Just Went Viral 65

Everyone Gets an Oscar (Why Video?) 65

3-2-1 Action! (Live Video) 69

Film School Just Found a Natural (Fully Edited Video) 71

There Are Weirder Ways to Learn (Webinars) 73

4. Hello, Is This Thing On? **77**

Your Commute Just Got Tons More Fun (Audio) 77

Radio's Making a Comeback, MTV! (Podcasts) 78

Just Read It to Me; I'm Busy (Audiobooks) 87

5. A Trillion Photos (of Beaches and Feet) **95**

I See Dead People (Why Visuals) 95

I'm No Ansel Adams, But I Have a Smartphone (Photos) 97

Honey, Just Show Me (Graphics) 98

Hipsters Do It, So I Definitely Won't (GIFs/Memes) 100

6. The Peanut Gallery Needs Some Love Too **105**

Little Bit of Everything in My Sights (Hodgepodge) 105

If It's Free, They Will Come (Contests and Giveaways) 107

Didn't Work during the Election, Might Work Now (Polls) 110

Do You Ever Stop Nagging? (Questions) 111

Party's Just Getting Started (Games) 112

Come on, Storyteller, Give Me Something (Stories) 113

Who Are Your Peeps? (Shout-outs) 114

Opinions Are Like...uh, Never Mind (Reviews) 115

Old School Is the New School (Email News) 118

7. Keep at It; You're Not Done Yet **133**

Bonus Material **139**

Bonus Material #1: Social Media Planning Guide and Tracker 140

Bonus Material #2: 162 Ideas for Digital Content Posts 143

Bonus Material #3: Hashtags 152

Bonus Material #4: Annual Holidays Calendar 156

Acknowledgments 171

About the Author 175

Introduction

Book marketing advice is available all over the internet, and most of it is so overwhelming that authors throw their hands up, scream, cry, give up, or just pay someone.

- You're on Facebook but not Twitter?
- Post to Twitter six times a day!
- Wait, Instagram is the place to be.
- Why don't you have a blog or a YouTube channel or a podcast?
- You must spend three hours a day marketing if you have a prayer of selling any books, because none of the Big Five publishers will take you without a platform.

- Facebook Ads! Google Ads! Amazon Ads!
- Get that email list up and running.
- Your website must be revamped.
- Do it all! Now!

Are you tossing your papers and giving me the evil eye yet? If every author did everything on this list, no books would ever get written—or sold.

Here's the deal: You do not have to do it all. You don't have to be on every platform, and you don't have to provide every type of content. What you do need to do is write a really good book (professionally edited with a professionally designed cover), build your platform, and find new followers or readers.

You need to do the platform building quickly and efficiently. I'm here to help you market your book in an effective and focused way. You won't be spread out all over the place shooting darts. You'll focus your energy on a social media platform you enjoy, and develop the content you like.

To start, you have to accept that, whether you are traditionally or self-published, you will have to do the bulk of your own marketing. I don't know if I consider that an unfair reality of the business or simply the reality. Publishing has historically been a saturated market, and those who've had commercial success have generally been willing to promote themselves and their books. Just ask Charles Dickens or Mark Twain. Even a basic marketing package with a major publishing house will require you to do some publicity and marketing.

Social media marketing for your book is about offering an authentic experience with you, the author. Whether you post to

Facebook six times a day or video your life on YouTube, the bottom line is you must offer the reader something they are not getting anywhere else. Do you know what that is? It's you.

Readers buy from people they know or think they know or their friends know. How do you get them to know you? Well, you create a space online for readers. In the industry, the professionals call it building your platform. I like to think of this more as building your community because that's what you're doing. You offer a place where a reader can pop into when they want to and get to know you. The "you" that you choose to share with those readers is completely up to you. I call it your public persona and discuss it in more detail in chapter 1.

One social media outlet is enough to get you started. Read that again, because I want to take away your stress. One social media outlet is enough to create a space online for your readers to get to know you. Chuck Wendig? Twitter. Jon Krakauer? Instagram. Make the content fun and interactive, and you're golden.

But What about Other Marketing?

Marketing absolutely involves more than social media. I advise all authors to build their marketing plans around the following four items:

- Design a static website with at least book information and links to social media.
- Build your email distribution list.
- Learn how to create effective Amazon ads.
- Start posting on one social media outlet with posts you enjoy.

You can build a website fairly easily on your own with WordPress, Weebly, Wix, or Squarespace. In the beginning, you just need to have a static page with little more than bio information. Readers expect it. The industry expects it. And, frankly, you need it. Everything you post to social media isn't exclusively yours and could be gone in a heartbeat. Remember MySpace? Google+? Your website is yours, and you own everything on it. If you want to blog a little or write articles and post them, that's good, too, but not necessary when just starting out.

The second step you need to take is to start building your email list. I go in-depth on this in chapter 5. Believe it or not, email is still the best way to contact people without paying for ads. Organic reach on social media is at an all-time low, but organic reach on email blows it out of the water. It's simple math, really.

Social media outlets want to make money, so unless you pay them for ads, your posts will be delivered to less than 5% of your followers. Email, on the other hand, is delivered to 75% of your list (it would be higher, but sometimes the emails end up in spam or bounced for whatever reason). Even if you buy ads on social media, you won't get that kind of reach.

You don't have to start sending emails until you are ready, but the time is now to set it up and start gathering the email addresses. Think about it like this—if you'd only used Google+ for your outreach and never collected your followers' email addresses, when it closed in the spring of 2019, you just lost all ability to reach those people. Had you gotten their email addresses, then you could still reach them.

Third. Learn everything you can about ads – Facebook and Amazon. Facebook has some of the best targeting data on the planet. That helps you focus your ad on the people more likely to read your book. You don't want to waste money on ads for readers who don't read your genre. Mark Dawson's *Mastering Simple Facebook Ads for Authors* is great. So is *Help! My Facebook Ads Suck* by Michael and Mal Cooper.

Amazon is a gigantic search engine. You know who uses it? People primed to buy stuff. You don't need to worry about producing your ads until a few months before you're ready to release the book. Until then, simply study as much as you can. Kindlepreneur.com is a helpful site to start, and Brian Meeks has a great book called *Mastering Amazon Ads.*

But, Social Media

The point of this book, however, is to help you learn how to use social media to your advantage. I know I just said organic reach is abysmal, but there are workarounds, and I'll get into all of them. Additionally, if you manage the workarounds, the power of social media can be harnessed to help you build that authentic experience readers are looking for.

People go to social media for the distraction. If you can build a fun, informative, entertaining distraction, readers will dig it and show up in droves. I'm here to teach you where to find those readers and how to create different types of content to attract them.

The rule of thumb for your content is if you enjoy creating it, keep doing it. Enthusiasm is contagious. If you try to produce content you don't like, that will show and turn folks off. Create a world you enjoy, and others will enjoy it too.

I want to dispel a nasty little rumor before we get started. You can't build a platform, grow an email list, or build a following in just ten minutes a day. Can't be done. That doesn't mean you have to spend hours on end doing it. The point of this book is to help you create your platform and find a following on social media effectively and efficiently, inevitably saving you time in the long run.

I plop myself in front of a movie and spend two or three hours on a Sunday afternoon scheduling all of my posts. I call it Platform Planning Sunday. It happens about once a month. Then, during the week, I spend thirty to forty-five minutes a day or every other day doing maintenance—commenting, following, retweeting, and so on. This is the essence of efficient platform building. Recognizing it will take a bit of time, and planning your posts will give you minutes back in your day because you won't be struggling with what to share.

In order to keep this task from taking over your life, you'll want to use social media management tools such as Buffer or Hootsuite. With these, you can create the content and schedule the day and time the post should show up on your outlet. These schedulers also allow you to create maintenance posts right there on the dashboard. If you don't use a scheduler, posting to social media just becomes a time suck.

If you can embrace the idea that you are now a business owner who will need to manage marketing in your day by using a scheduler, posting the kind of content you enjoy, I promise it won't feel like such a chore.

Why Listen to Me?

Because I've spent my entire career in marketing and communications, and I care about your success. I want you to have the skills to market your books without wanting to die doing it. I wrote this book because I want to help writers feel less overwhelmed, and I have years of experience and education to back it up.

I know some writers balk at giving you a lot of credentials, and I hate talking about myself, but I do think that, since I'm new on the scene, you should know a little about me. Since 2001, I have had the most incredible job. It's so fun to be a professional communicator, and there is always something new to learn. We get to communicate, market, publicize, and reach people who may or may not want to be reached. I party-planned for the US Ambassador to Portugal. I managed location production for Hollywood filmmakers and got to have lunch with a famous late-night television host (I can't tell you who, but we ate Taco Bell, and he's really funny!). I answered international press questions about peace in South Korea, open press in Serbia, and humanitarian aid in Sudan. But what probably makes me more qualified for book marketing is the time I've spent providing research opportunities for writers, professors, documentary filmmakers, and members of Congress.

While I still do this type of communication, I shifted my focus to book marketing after meeting some really wonderful authors in 2012. The Pikes Peak Writers Conference is held every spring in Colorado Springs. I was introduced to a multitude of writers—nonfiction, fantasy, romance, thriller, cookbook, memoir—and being around their creativity really struck a chord with me, one I hadn't felt since my fiction-writing days of college.

One of my favorite Pikes Peak Writers nicknamed her home "Off Kilter" and changed Google maps to reflect it. Isn't that kind of originality just so fun to be around?

But something else they introduced me to was their anxiety about marketing. "I just wanna write" was heard so frequently it should be on a bumper sticker. It was pretty clear to me that I could offer marketing advice to this community and hopefully ease some of that anxiety. I mean, I love this stuff, and seriously, if I couldn't figure out book marketing with all my years of experience, we were all screwed.

So, I attended every workshop, conference, and retreat I could. I am a member of the Public Relations Society of America and began attending book marketing courses. Over the years, I've coached countless writers on effective social media and have taught numerous classes on the subject. The bottom line is I want to share that with you to make your life a little easier, because the more books we have in the world, the happier it is!

What Could You Possibly Get Here You Can't Get Elsewhere?

Honestly, most of what you'll find in this book is scattered all over the internet. But do you have hours to comb through all that and figure out what really works? I know you'd rather be writing. So, I dug through the mountain of data, tested my own ideas, and applied what I know to design this book. It gives a new or struggling author a good foundation to establish a community on social media.

This foundation will increase your followers, find your readers, and grow your email list. All of this is with the objective to build your author platform and help you sell books efficiently and effectively.

Throughout the book, I use *post* and *digital content* interchangeably, but what you need to know is that digital content is anything you post online. Whether that's a video or photo, a meme or poll, it's all digital content. As you read the book, keep the following principles in mind:

- You must plan. Plan. Plan. Plan. Without a plan, you'll flounder. It's that simple. Pantsers, stop squirming. This isn't plotting a story. It's planning your book's marketing future. And you want your baby set up well out in the world, right?
- You must define your reader. As much as we'd like to think every person wants to read our book, that's just not the case. Your reader is someone special and s/he needs to be forefront in every single post, tweet, message, pin, snap, and even book you create. I don't mean "buy my book" content either. I mean you need to provide something interesting and fun for the reader. Create a space they want to be.
- You'll learn about video, podcasting, photos, memes, infographics, polls, giveaways, questions, and other types of posts for social media.
    - ☐ Do not incorporate every single thing I teach you.
    - ☐ Do pick one type and become really good at it.
    - ☐ Do pick more than one type if you're comfortable posting content.
- You will learn about five major social media outlets: Facebook, YouTube, Instagram, Twitter, and Pinterest. I leave out Snapchat because it's simply not set up for business just yet, and its user base is still relatively small compared to other outlets.
    - ☐ Do not use every single one of these outlets unless you're comfortable with posting content and efficient with a scheduler. (Hint: Even if you are comfortable, you still don't need to be on them all.)

- Do use at least one social media platform plus a website. (Hint: Facebook is still the number-one social media outlet, but Instagram is growing fast.)

- You will learn about what works on social media.
    - And you do need to learn it and keep up with the annual research (resources provided at www.jenniferlovettherbranson.com/SMforAuthorsResourcesforStudy, don't worry).
    - By keeping up with trends and successes, you can plan which type of content to use on which social media outlet.
    - Go slowly and learn so you aren't overwhelmed.

I've divided the book into seven chapters:

Chapter 1 is the foundation for every other section. It covers why you need digital content, how to develop your public persona, and how to understand your reader.

Chapter 2 discusses each of the social media outlets and best practices for using them. I get into best posting times for each outlet and some tools to help you post faster and smarter.

Chapters 3 through 6 explain the type of content you'll post and specifically how to create each type of post. Chapter 3 details why you need to consider video content, what it is, and how to do it.

Chapter 4 explains the same thing for audio content such as podcasts and audiobooks. Chapter 5 gets into visual content—photos and graphics, GIFs, and memes. Chapter 6 is a hodgepodge of other ideas that focuses on contests, giveaways, email news, polls, and reviews.

The final and seventh part of this book has a repository of Bonus Material tools to focus your marketing and help you plan. You'll find tons of ideas, quirky holidays to note, hashtags to experiment with, and a checklist to help you plan. Trust me, if I do say so myself, this Bonus Material alone is worth the price of this book.

My last piece of advice is this: Ask for help anytime. Whether you're just starting out and need some advice or you've been at this a while and are stuck, email me, message me, or shoot me a tweet. Make sure to sign up for my free email that gives monthly tips and keeps you updated on statistics you need to be successful. Think of me as your marketing partner.

Email: writernationjen@gmail.com

Twitter: twitter.com/writernationjen

Sign up for Writer Nation email with free tips and advice at www.thewriternation.com.

Peace & Prose, & Happy Writing!

Jen

"The Secret of Getting Ahead is Getting Started"

—Mark Twain

It's Been Years, but I Still Don't Know Jack

Social media has been around forever. It's no longer new, and it hasn't been the longer that thing the kids do in a decade. Social media marketing is a billion-dollar industry and extremely effective in selling products. But just because you use Facebook or have Instagram doesn't mean you know how to market on those platforms.

This book teaches you how to do that. Have you heard the term "building your platform"? An author's platform is the experience you offer the reader online and in your books. Prepublished marketing is about community and relationship building. If you create a quality environment for potential readers, you'll have a platform to create a buzz for when you are ready to publish. Early published marketing (for authors with a book just out) is tapping into that community you've built to expand the buzz and sell books.

Do you know who your reader is? You need to define that person. Do you know who you want to be online? You also need to define that person. Your public persona is what people will know about you. Do you know what type of content you enjoy creating and which social media site you enjoy using? I'm going to talk about all that because this is the basis of your social media marketing plan that will enable you to build your platform.

"Word of mouth is still the most effective form of promotion," said Michael Larsen, a super-agent and founder of Larsen-Pomada Literary Agents, at the San Francisco Writers Conference in 2017. That has always been the case and will continue to be the case. The deal is that word of mouth has moved from the water cooler to online. That's where your platform comes in.

I attend a lot of writers' conferences throughout the year. One of the more frequent questions I get is, "What am I supposed to post to social media?" I've seen frustration rise throughout conversations when we start talking about social media and marketing a brand.

Frequently, writers are told to start building their brand before, during, and after writing a book, and to do that, they must be on social media. All social media. Every day. Several times a day. I agree with some of this advice. I do believe you can never start too early when building your brand.

But does that mean you need to be on six different social media outlets, posting relentlessly? No. I am definitely in the camp that says a website and one social media outlet is enough while you're building a brand and writing your first set of books. I know you'd rather be writing, and, frankly, books sell books. So, the more books you have to sell, the more likely you'll sell the other books. None of this is possible without a plan.

At a Lady Jane's Salon in Bethesda, Maryland, a writer friend and I got into a deep discussion about her frustration with social media. The conversation went something like this:

"I can totally help you with your marketing," I said. "What's going on?"

"I have four books out," she began. "And I'm having zero luck with my Facebook page. I don't want to even try Twitter."

"How often do you post?" I asked. "And what type of posts?"

"Once or twice a day," she said. "I do everything the experts"—she air-quotes with her fingers—"tell me to do. Questions, polls, pictures. And I'm getting no traction, and I'm ready to ditch. Can you just tell me why should I be on Facebook if it doesn't work?"

This is a conversation I've had multiple times with tired, frustrated writers, and it drove the reason for this book. Creating quality content online requires a plan and a good idea of what attracts users. I want to help you do that. Our objective in building your platform is to create a place where your readers will feel special and valued.

Keep this idea front and center with every single thing you do online. We're building a community for readers to get to know you and your work. People jump on social media to be distracted. In order to do this, you first have to figure out what your platform is.

Online Marketing: A No-Brainer

According to Pew Research, in 2018, nearly 90% of Americans admitted they are online. In addition, 70% of Americans identify themselves as readers. This is even as other forms of entertainment have jumped in popularity and surpassed reading as an American pastime. That being said, if you want to reach readers, you will have an easier time finding them online than offline.

Goodreads was built by two Stanford students for just this purpose—to reach readers. More than 30,000 book reviews are posted *daily*, and 17 million books are added to members' Want-to-Read shelves every month. Those numbers tell you readers are paying attention.

In addition to the Goodreads data regarding online readers, Facebook boasts more than 653 million users who also list reading as a favorite pastime or interest. Of the top two fiction genres, 123 million said they liked reading mystery fiction, and 92 million said romance novels. That's a lot of readers.

A multitude of different surveys in the last three years found that readers buy books from authors they know or authors they've been referred to—back to that word-of-mouth concept, the new water cooler. The Alliance of Independent Authors found 68% of their respondents bought books because the author was well known to the reader, and 82% said they bought a book by an author they already knew. Other surveys showed similar results.

Our goal is to help you become the author people know or the author they're talking about. If you aren't online, it's going to be really difficult for readers to get to know you.

For potential readers to get to know you online, you must produce content. Digital content spreads because it inspires a community.

You can't just post whatever and expect it to attract a following. You are not writing books for yourself. You are writing them to inspire a community to get to know you. If you're writing fiction, that community should encourage your readers to get to know your characters. If you're writing nonfiction, it should motivate your readers to get to know your field. To find those readers and build that community, you should employ digital content that inspires people to talk about it. That's how news spreads, and you the author benefit by increasing the numbers in your community.

Caution: the content should benefit the reader. Bombarding them with requests for information or book buying links will turn them off. This is a relationship on their terms. If they like what you're offering, they'll stick around. If they think they are being "sold to" every time they see your content, they'll bolt.

Author Platform: You the Author

Your author platform is the public persona you wish to project and the world of your books. That's it. People buy books from people they know or think they know. That makes you part of the commodity in the business you are building. Yes, *you* the author are part of the package deal. Don't let that freak you out, because you get to decide what you reveal.

Think about what you want readers to know about you. Don't say "nothing" because that's not going to work. You have likes and dislikes, interests and hobbies. To start, pick two personal facts that you are willing to share with others. What do you want them to know about you? What part of you are you willing to share with strangers? What keeps readers interested and you comfortable?

For example, I love Alabama football. I don't mean that I watch it every now and then and might be able to pick the head coach out of a lineup. I mean that I know who every starter and their backups are. I know who the coordinators and their assistants are. I watch the professional combine to see how graduates are doing in their NFL tryouts, and I can't wait for my July editions of *Athlon* and *Lindy* magazines so I can see how our players are shaping up for the new season.

Everyone who knows me knows I have strong opinions on Alabama football and how fun it is to be a part of the Southern culture in general. I even warn new Facebook followers that Saturdays in the fall get rowdy on my page. What's awesome about sports, and college football in particular, is how it brings people together, and I have quite a cohesive community during the season.

I also love to travel. As of the writing of this book, I've been to forty different countries and plan to visit a hundred more before I die. I post pictures of cultural sites, beaches, mountains, jungles, locals, food, whatever I find interesting and compelling about the location. Sharing the way other cultures live is really fun for me, and my followers seem to get a kick out of it.

For instance, I posted an *ajumma* (Korean for elderly aunt) working in the rice paddies to show people how rice gets to the table. I also shared a photo of the giant Bodhisattva overlooking Da Nang beach in Vietnam because most people I know have never been to Vietnam.

From Europe, I posted my opinions on all the sites we read about in middle-school history class—the Roman Colosseum, the Eiffel Tower, Anne Frank's house in Amsterdam, the Louvre. By the way, Leonardo da Vinci's *Mona Lisa* is tiny and way overrated.

A word on privacy and security for travel posts. I don't post which hotels I stay at until I come home, and I don't post my itinerary, ever. One year for Christmas, we went to Costa Rica for two weeks, and I turned off every electronic device I owned. I took a stand-alone camera instead of using my phone, and rather than posting pictures in real time, I waited until I got home and posted every day for two weeks.

When I'm on vacation, I want to stay on vacation. I don't want to worry about security or marketing. So, I relax. I take photos of people and places I think are interesting. Before I leave, however, I do plan out my regular social media posts and use a scheduler so I don't feel compelled to do marketing while I'm on vacation. More on schedulers later.

I also post movie reviews. I love the movies! My daughter and I see a lot of them. Christmas is our favorite time of year when we typically see five or six movies during the school break at the theater with big bags of popcorn, huge drinks, and SweeTarts. When I get home, I write a review so my friends and followers will know if the movie is worth seeing or not. The reviews keep me writing, which I love, and offer something to the community.

Posting about hobbies or one or two quirks is true for other writers. Sweet Southern romance author Mary Kay Andrews shares antiquing finds and stories. Spy thriller author Barry Eisler, former CIA operative, posts about politics. Hot Hollywood romance author MK Meredith is known for her love of peanut butter. Rom-com author Pippa Grant uses aliases when talking about the antics of her kids using aliases and photos without faces. I have one friend who discusses interesting anecdotes from riders in his taxi.

As a fiction writer, one thing you are *not* doing is creating a writer persona for other writers. Unless you are writing nonfiction books on the publishing world, your public persona is not a teacher of writers. I know we want to share our knowledge, but you are creating something for your readers, not your colleagues.

Whether you are a fiction writer or a nonfiction writer, your public persona needs to include the human side, too. Let people get to know you. So, think about you: What do you like, what are you comfortable discussing with others, and what topics bring you joy that you can share with your followers? This is your public persona.

The point is that we don't need social media to invade every part of our lives. We control what we put out and when. What I post is innocuous—football, travel, and movie reviews—but it's something I'm known for, and people enjoy. I do not talk about my day job much because that could cause too many problems, and I don't post about my family much, either, to protect their privacy.

I don't want you to feel compelled to share every single part of your life or to be turned off because you feel you need to. You don't. You get to decide what you share. You get to decide what your platform will be. If sharing something makes you uncomfortable, then do not make that part of your public persona.

Brainstorm a list of hobbies, activities, likes, and dislikes you have and look at the list. What three items or interests could you take from that list and feel comfortable sharing with the world? That is the start of your platform.

The other half of this platform is your books. They are a treasure trove of a place to excavate for ideas and for helping you determine your platform. (The nice thing about your fictional characters is they don't have to worry about privacy issues.) Go through your main character, minor characters, and antagonist.

- What are their jobs?
- What are their hobbies?
- What do they hate? Love?

- What activities are in their daily habits?
- Do they own pets? Have kids? Take care of parents?

Think about your setting:

- Where is it?
- What is the culture of the town, city, country?
- What foods do they eat?
- What activities are prevalent in the place?

Now, what about the themes and messages:

- Love conquers all?
- Big city versus small-town life?
- Family first?
- Good guys always win?
- CIA black ops guys with unique skills?

All of the answers give you room to play with your posts because you are introducing your characters and your books to your followers, whether it's a book in progress or one already published. You can use this material to create a community online for readers. If it's a series, that's even better because you can build a thread around the interesting facts about the location and families involved.

If you're a nonfiction author, think about what you're trying to teach someone with your book:

- Define the problem or question you're solving in your book.

- Develop the reasons why the problem/question exists.
- Create a list of possible solutions.
- Brainstorm a list of why you are the expert to help readers solve this problem or answer the question.
- Explain how the solutions work.
- Explain what the reader must do to implement the solutions.

This technique works for memoirists, biographers, historians, anyone writing a nonfiction book, because they all exist to teach a reader something. Once you figure out what that is, you've basically defined the intent. Your questions will almost always be how or why:

- Who were the law enforcement officers who brought down Bonnie and Clyde, and how did they do it?
- How do I fix the leak under the sink?
- What was Roosevelt's reasoning for staying out of World War II at the beginning?
- Why did the United States invade Iraq?
- What started the bank meltdown in 2008?
- Who discovered the polio vaccine and how?

After this is done, you need to define your reader.

Who Reads This Stuff?

Before you get into posting anything anywhere, you need to do some research and learn two basic facts: Who are your readers and what are the norms of your genre? A hard fact of life is that you are not everyone's cup of tea. That's okay, because you are someone's cup of tea. I know we'd all like everyone to read our work but think about your own reading habits.

I love thrillers but hate horror. I enjoy reading historical romance but not urban fantasy. It's not personal to the author. It's simply preference. There is an audience out there for you. A reader who will love everything you write. Your job is to find them. In order to do that you need to define them first.

Who is your reader?

- Male or female or LGBTQ?
- Age?
- Where do they live?
- What do they like to do?
- What types of careers do they lean toward?

Define this person. Give him or her a name. My reader is Bailey, a male or female author with a day job, probably over thirty-five and finally taking the time to write the novel or novels s/he's always had in her/his head. When s/he was a kid, s/he played make-believe and always had her/his nose in a book. These days, Bailey attends at least one writers' workshop or conference a year, belongs to the local writers' organization, and tries to write when everyone else is asleep.

S/he might have a subscription to *Writer's Digest* magazine and has probably finished the first novel but isn't quite sure what to do next. Bailey might actually have two or three novels written and has decided to hire an editor and really give this writing life a go. S/he still isn't sure what to do about marketing but is willing to learn. S/he's on Facebook and Twitter, but may or may not have branched out to Instagram yet.

This tells me I can find Bailey on mainstream social media and in writers' groups on Facebook.

So, who is *your* reader? Take a few minutes and brainstorm him/her. Write it down. Not to be repetitive, but who your reader is not is other writers. There is a wonderfully nice tendency in our writing career field to provide hacks, guides, lists, or whatever for other writers. It truly is a nice gesture, and I know you want to share what you've learned, but for your platform, you need to create a niche for readers of your work. Focus on what world or community you are providing to your particular reader. Now, if you're writing nonfiction books on the publishing industry, ignore everything you just read and go for it. But if you're not, hyperfocus your platform on your reader and what your reader expects of you and your work.

Once you figure out who your reader is, you have to understand what that reader expects when looking online for information about new books and authors in your genre. The norms of your genre are important for you because they brand your book for that genre. If you've written 200,000 words and are calling it rom-com, it is time to rethink that. Readers look for certain customs or similarities when they look for a particular genre.

Rand Fishkin is the CEO and co-founder of SparkToro, a company that helps people do better marketing. Rand was named among the 30 Best Young Tech Entrepreneurs Under 30 by *Businessweek*, and he's been featured in *Newsweek* and the *New York Times*. He recommends five ways to help get your content amplified and promoted online:

- Find successful content in your niche.
- Find what is being shared.

- Find who is sharing.
- Copy what works for them.
- Build relationships with those who can help.

What he's saying is you must do market research and understand the genre or niche you're trying to break into. There are certain norms and expectations of your market that readers have. While it's good to break out of molds, think of this as the structure of genre fiction. Readers expect a three-act structure or hero's journey in much the same way potential customers expect a store to be laid out in an organized manner that makes it easy to find all the soaps together, or the nails with the hammers.

To understand the structure of the market, ask yourself these questions: Who are the major players in your genre? What are they posting? What are they posting that works better than others? Look at the midlevel authors too who are doing well but are maybe not as well-known as James Patterson, Stephen King, or Nora Roberts. What are those folks posting that works?

Now, look at your content. Is it so far outside the box that people won't understand the genre you're writing in or does it fit right in? Is it slightly edgier to stand out a bit? Think of this more like different twists on tropes. In genre fiction writing, tropes are "stereotype" stories or plot conventions. In the romance genre, examples are: secret baby, long-lost love, enemies to friends. Romance writers build interesting and new stories around those tropes and again, that's what readers expect. Does your book seem similar to what the industry is doing but still reflect your own personal style? In essence, that's how you focus your content and stand out.

Give 'em All the Feels

Once you've figured out who your reader is and are confident that your book matches what they are looking for in your genre, it's time to go out and bring them to you. The reason I am a big Facebook advocate (and I haven't always been) is because it has an enormous amount of data to help you find a following.

Because Facebook bought Instagram, that data now flows across both platforms. Users let Facebook know all the time what they like with the like button, but also with their About sections. This trove is invaluable to someone trying to build a following. You can find readers who like authors similar to you.

To build a following, you need to make the potential reader feel something. Make them cry. Make them laugh. Make them fall in love or scare them to death. For nonfiction, make them wonder and delight and hope at your information. Turn on a lightbulb. For both types of writing, gut-punch them into submission with all the feels you can manage.

To do that, your content needs to meet one of these three objectives: educate, inform, or entertain. Posts that educate, inform, or entertain should also accomplish one of three results: reinforce a belief, refute an argument, or renew a discussion. This formula is how you get readers to feel and to think.

The first type of objective is to educate your followers on something you really enjoy doing. Think back to your platform. What are your hobbies and those of your characters? Needlepoint lessons, CrossFit workouts, hiking trails, glassblowing videos—all of these are fun activities to educate your community. Let's look at how your post can meet the three results:

- Reinforce what people already know: Only grandmothers do needlepoint (kidding). CrossFit workouts will kill you (also kidding). Hiking trails all have bears (well, in Appalachia they do).
- Refute an argument: Grandmas aren't the only ones who needlepoint. CrossFit workouts really are for everyone. Hiking trails are all groomed and available for every level hiker.
- Renew a discussion: Why you should take up needlepoint. Why CrossFit is good for every level of athlete. Why the Appalachian Trail should be rerouted.

The second type of objective is to inform. This sort of post discusses an event you want to let people know about. Are you attending a retreat, conference, or workshop? Do you have a speaking gig somewhere? What are you doing? More importantly, what's the progress of your book? Those are also inform-type posts.

- Reinforce the dates and locations.
- Refute someone who got something wrong. I call this one "correcting the record" politely so you don't sound like a jerk.
- Renew a discussion about the event. Ask questions about it. Who's going? What are they looking forward to?

Finally, a post that entertains is just that, entertaining—the third type of objective. Charles Dickens said, "There is nothing in the world so irresistibly contagious as laughter and good humor." Make your posts something fun. Tell jokes. Deliver games or trivia. Share hilarious videos. Pull out fun activities going on with your community or in your life. I know it sounds funny that you can reinforce, refute, or renew a post meant to entertain, but you can.

- Reinforce a belief: Skydiving is awesome. Post a video.
- Refute an argument: Coke is better than Pepsi. Period.
- Renew a discussion: What is the best series on Netflix right now?

I want to emphasize one point when you are thinking about what you are posting and why. Opinions, your opinions, matter. Remember your platform? This is where you utilize your platform. People engage because they have an emotional reaction to something you said. That is not to say you need to weigh in on politics or religion, but if you don't have opinions on anything, then your posts are boring, vanilla, and people will go elsewhere. If you're just parroting what everyone else is saying, then you aren't providing worthy content. You want to give an opinion to evoke emotion because then they'll talk. If you can get people talking, that is gold.

YOU ASKED FOR IT... *Quick* TIPS

Here are my down-and-dirty, no kidding, tidbits of information. Do these to get started:

Do not get started without a plan. This one is important, so I'm going to say it again. Do not get started without a plan. This is where most folks go wrong. They slap content up on social media without a thought of who the audience is or how they should be reached. They don't think about who their reader is or how often they should post to generate engagement.

Know your reader. This step is also vital. Use the sections in this chapter to help you figure out who your reader is. How do you find that reader? Where? When? Use the planning guide and tracker in the Bonus Material section to help you gain perspective. This guide helps you define your goals and think through your plan. Then use the tracker or an online scheduler to actually plan out your social media posts because it's an efficient use of your time.

WRAP UP

- Develop your public persona.
- Research your genre and its marketing trends.
- Define your reader.
- Use the Rule of Thirds when generating content.

"Stretching yourself thin is a damn waste of time. Marketing laziness breeds efficiency & focus."

—Me, Jennifer Lovett Herbranson

This Internet Is Huge

Too Many Social Media Platforms

This book is built around tips, tools, and ideas to help you logistically create and build that content. Now that you know what your public persona is and who your audience is and the purpose behind effective content, it's time to start posting. Where do you start? Start where you are comfortable. If Facebook is intuitive to you and you enjoy it, then that's where you start. If you hate it but like to talk to people, try podcasting. It doesn't matter where you start, you just need to start. I started with a Facebook Group of friends.

For the sake of this book, and your sanity, I'm going to focus on only the five major social media sites that will drive the most traffic to your website, blog, or Amazon Author Page: Facebook, YouTube, Instagram, Twitter, and Pinterest.

I'm not a fan of chasing the latest shiny object because, until it shows itself to be sustainable, it's a waste of time. You need to focus on writing books. You only have a limited amount of time to write, and we're trying to maximize that as much as possible. That being said, for newbies, pick one of these social media outlets and become proficient at using it for the most engagement.

For those ready to step it up, design a variety of content. Find what works for you. Keep in mind, you are not hard-selling your reader to buy your book. You are also not trying to make best friends with your reader. You are creating an online space a reader will find interesting; one that hopefully will compel them to jump on board your author train.

The most important aspect of your social media presence is that it is fruitful for the reader and for you. Don't waste your time on outlets you hate or designing content you don't find compelling. Additionally, don't stretch yourself thin. Laser-focus on building a strong followership, however that works for you.

You don't necessarily need to expand to a million platforms, but you might choose one more particular to your target reader. Facebook can reach just about everyone, but you'd find more crafty, upper-income women on Pinterest, and more males interested in sci-fi or fantasy on YouTube.

The next section discusses each of the social media sites and how to use them.

Facebook

There is no argument that Facebook is the most dominating social media channel out there with more than two billion users—all demographics, all ages (including teenagers, although their daily use is much higher on Instagram, YouTube, and Snapchat.) While its daily numbers in the United States leveled off from 2016 to 2018, they actually grew in 2019, according to Pew Research Center's May 2019 study "10 facts about Americans and Facebook." Americans spend almost an hour on the site every day. Across all platforms, Facebook has the highest daily user base of any social media channel around the world. Making that statistic even more interesting is that out of that daily user base, more than 1 billion of them speak English. This is important to you because, even if you aren't thinking about publishing books in other countries, you will probably get around to that one day.

Publishing your English novel in Ireland, the UK, Australia, and New Zealand would yield you higher returns, and all those folks are on Facebook too. While I don't think the privacy scandals will hurt Facebook in the long run, keep an eye on this platform as more than 40% of Americans admitted to taking a break from it at some point in 2018.

Facebook changed its algorithm in January 2018 to encourage more interaction with family and friends and less with businesses, even if you've followed the page. I'm fairly certain they changed it to increase ad revenue, because the only way you can increase your following on a Facebook Page is with ads. Yet, I digress. This new algorithm is great if you run a Facebook Group, or you use your Facebook Profile as the platform for your readers. These two platforms allow you to grow followers organically. The more interaction your posts generate, the better exposed your posts will be.

How to use Facebook. Facebook has three ways to further your brand: a profile, group, or page.

Your Facebook Profile is just that—the normal page you see and use when you log in to Facebook. You can simply use your profile as a way to friend everyone. You'll max out at 5,000. Most people do not do this because they actually do use Facebook to reach friends and family. If you're planning on reserving your profile for personal use, I recommend you do not use it for your writer business. Don't create a separate profile for your author self either. Managing multiple profiles is against Facebook rules, and if you're caught, they'll close your account.

You can also utilize Facebook Groups. The new algorithm actually encourages interaction from groups over brands, so organic growth is easier with groups. At the end of 2018, 200 million users considered themselves members of "meaningful" Facebook Groups, which means the group had become part of their daily interactions.

A group can be a community or fan club or street team or whatever you want it to be. The type of information here can be considered exclusive for the members: extra chapters of your book, ongoing progress of the current book, character interviews, or book club discussions. Go back to your platform: What community do you want to build? Groups can be the place to do that.

Facebook Pages are the professional, business pages you create and use for your writing career. Here's the deal with pages: You need a profile to run a page, but the page will never show your connection to your profile. Why does this matter? Two words—pen name.

If you write under a pseudonym, the page won't give away that you are behind it. If you don't use a pen name, the page is still important because this is the professional career page you need to advertise to the world you are a writer. It's where you post all the stuff going on with you—signings, talks, conferences, book launches, and so on. This is also where you put out that persona I talked about earlier. Once you're ready to start posting, you need to think about growth.

Your Facebook Page will reach about 3% of your followers organically. If you want to reach more, you'll need to buy ads. This is not necessarily a bad idea because, with a good ad buy, you can target audiences for different results. If your book is ready to come out, purchase an ad that specifically targets readers in your genre. If you are list building for your email news, create an ad aimed at anyone who would be interested in your platform.

A word about ads. The page is the only place you can build ads. Those ads can be made from your digital content, so it's important to build quality posts here as well. Go into Manage Ads, and the setup is user-friendly. Ads are beyond the scope of this book, but the bottom line is, if you want to advertise a book or your email news or even the page itself beyond your followers and group members, you need a Facebook Page to do it.

Best practices. As of the writing of this book, the best posts on Facebook were Instagram photos and live Facebook video. A close second are videos uploaded directly to the site. Besides those, any post that encourages interaction will do well. Think of this when you develop your ads, too. If you're advertising a book release or sale, this content is worth considering. Facebook changed its algorithm again in June 2019. Do not use phrases like "comment below" or "like for a freebie" or anything that overtly encourages interaction. Facebook wants you to build that organically, so asking questions that provoke a response will keep you on the Facebook good girl/boy list.

Analytics. Make sure you look at your analytics for your group or page at least weekly. Facebook has a rich analytics stash that can help you figure out when your followers are most likely to engage with your posts, and which posts garner the most comments, likes, and shares. This data will help you plan your future posts.

You can find this information for your group under Group Insights, or at the top of your Facebook Page, click Insights. My group garners the most interaction on Thursdays, and the best post on my page was about book launches. This information can help you discover what makes your followers most engaged. Use that to help you plan future posts.

YouTube

YouTube has shown itself to be a juggernaut not only in social media, but also as a search engine tool. It is the second most-used social media outlet worldwide, behind Facebook, of course, and boasts more than 1.5 billion monthly users. It ranks higher than Facebook and Google as the most-used search engine outlet. These three platforms flip-flop year after year for the top spot, so it's worth paying attention to all of these in terms of your online and digital marketing. It probably helps that YouTube is owned by Google.

With fifty million creators, there are 300 hours of video uploaded to YouTube every day. Thirty million users watch those videos for at least an hour every single day. According to Omnicore Agency, women are watching beauty videos, and men watch sports shows.

One interesting fact about YouTube is that 80% of its users reside outside the United States. The site has services in ninety-one countries and in eighty languages. This is essential information for writers who plan to sell their books in an overseas market—a practice I highly recommend. In the United States, however, Pew Research discovered in 2018 that 73% of American adults use YouTube, another compelling statistic for book marketers.

YouTube is more likely to be used by men than women at a 4:1 ratio. This is good for authors of any fiction genre, but mainly books that don't involve romance. Writers of genres that attract more males will probably find more readers on YouTube, but that isn't to say using the platform is futile for those aimed at women. Anyone who enjoys making videos should absolutely be on YouTube, either creating a following on the channel or using it as a repository to post videos to other platforms.

How to use YouTube. As a writer, you want to create videos that teach, inspire, educate, or inform. You can read a section of your books. Create a 360-degree look into a location that inspired your book's setting. Build a tour of your writing world. Book trailers, interviews, and news are also ideas that work. YouTube won't sell a whole lot of books, but it will continue to create a connection and relationship with your readers. Remember, readers buy books from people they think they know. Videos are a great way for them to get to know you.

When you think about marketing on YouTube, you need to think about video length. Unless you are creating a niche channel that teaches or informs (think makeup tips or travel tours), remember this: Viewers who watched a video ad to a full thirty seconds were twenty-three times more likely to engage with that video, meaning follow, subscribe, share, or comment.

If you can do both, that's even better. One way to do that is to create a how-to series with tips. Figure out what you can create a series from in thirty seconds or less and start now. Brandwatch reported in January 2019 that searches for these kinds of videos increase 70% year after year. For fiction writers, use whatever career or hobby your main character has and create videos for that. The key here is to create videos for the reader, bring them into your world, or help them get to know you as an author.

A word about ads. YouTube has three types of ads available, and you must go through Google AdWords to set it up. Did I mention Google owns YouTube? Once you've created your video, go to AdWords and click Campaign, then Video. Follow the instructions from there. It's a click per view system, and you're bidding for views. You also have the ability to target your audience with keywords, phrases, or even websites. If you're unsure about a marketing video for you or your books, check out Wistia or Animoto to help you.

Best practices. Figure out your channel niche. What will this channel do for you? If you want to create a channel people consistently come back to, define what it is. If you're using it simply to hold your videos and post on other sites, this isn't as important. As with any video, make sure the first ten seconds of your video are totally rocking. Think of this like the first page of your book. If you're doing too much setup, backstory or intro, people will punch off of it. Get to the action quickly.

Create a channel trailer so people will know what to expect when they visit your site. If you create a series, the videos can be progressively longer but make sure to post consistently. If you don't like videos or aren't interested in producing them, don't. Your displeasure will come across, and the channel will fade over time anyway. Focus on what brings you joy.

Analytics. On the analytics page, YouTube provides several analytics categories good for your data analysis and research: how long someone watches your video (if they click off early, you're not getting to the point fast enough); how many people clicked on your videos, and engagement (likes, comments, shares, for example). All of this information should help inform your next video or ad idea.

Instagram

Instagram is simply blowing up these days. Now owned by Facebook for a cool $1 billion, it is the third most-used social media platform out there, behind Facebook and YouTube. In April 2019, Instagram boasted over one billion active monthly users. Of those billion users, 500 million are active every single day and like more than four billion posts each day. That's an incredible amount of usage.

The most active age group on the platform is twenty-five to thirty-four years old. And 70% of Americans aged eighteen to twenty-four, an age group more associated with Snapchat, admit to being active on Instagram as well. That being said, only a third of Americans said they used the platform in a poll in late 2018. I'd expect that to grow over time.

A couple of statistics are telling for a business owner: 70% of American businesses use Instagram, and 80% of all Instagram accounts follow at least one business. This data indicates businesses see the commercial viability of the platform, and the users seem to indicate they are okay with that, at least for now.

How to use Instagram. To use Instagram, you have to understand that the platform is not social networking like Facebook or Twitter. Instagram is all about the pics and videos. And they can't be crappy pics. They need to be high-quality photos. The artsier, the better. Try to stay away from memes or at least don't post them every day. Those should serve a specific purpose. Make sure to post your face as often as you're comfortable. Photos with your face on them will yield more interaction than those without. When it comes to video, the shorter, the better.

Videos have a 40% higher engagement rate than photos, but I wouldn't expect Facebook to turn Instagram into YouTube or Vine or Periscope anytime soon. Right now, Instagram limits videos to one minute or disappearing live video in the Stories section. I recommend posting videos once or twice a week, or even once every so often for now, and concentrate on photos. If you connect your Instagram to Facebook, those photos and videos will show prominently in the Facebook feed because Facebook wants to push its own asset.

Grow your following by following users, the same way you do on Twitter, but you don't need to worry about the follower-to-following ratio. Instagram doesn't penalize you for out-following your follower number like Twitter does. So, find a user you like and look at their followers. Follow the ones you think will follow you back or will help you create the kind of experience you are looking for on Instagram.

A word about ads. To buy ads on Instagram, you need to have a Facebook Page and an Instagram business account. It's no big deal to create a business account or turn yours into one. When you create the ad campaign, it will ask you if you want to advertise on Facebook and Instagram or just one of the sites—which you choose is really dependent on the audience you're trying to reach. If I'm building an email list, I use Facebook only. If I am trying to build a following, I'll use both. Then follow the instructions. Audience targeting is one of the best features of Instagram and Facebook ads. To learn more about your audience, look at your analytics.

Best practices. Used to be that the common practice was to post one photo a day. Now you can get away with three as long as they are quality photos. Use hashtags, a lot of them. Hashtags galore! Instagram isn't as restrictive about hashtag usage as Twitter. As a matter of fact, the platform allows up to thirty, but make sure to put them in the comments rather than in the caption and don't use the same ones all the time. To figure out which hashtags, think about the topic. What are the themes and messages of your brand, your book, and your world that you can use to exploit a hashtag?

For instance, John Grisham could use #legal #legalthriller #courtroomdrama. Nora Roberts could use #fairy #magic #romance. Create hashtags from your own content and use them. If you're having trouble deciding which hashtags to use, check out authors in your genre and see which hashtags they are using. For a reference of writer hashtags, see the Bonus Material #3: Hashtags section.

Analytics. In order to use Instagram analytics, you need to convert your account to a Business Profile. Once you do that, click on Insights. You can track engagement, interactions, impressions, as well as audience demographics and how well your posts are performing.

Twitter

I love Twitter. It's one of my favorite places on the internet. I've met all kinds of people on Twitter. It has more than 300 million users, which doesn't compare to Facebook, but according to Pew Research, the people on Facebook are not typically on Twitter as well.

You'll discover a massive Twitter underworld of writers, agents, publishers, editors, and publicists just waiting for you to find them. Agents actually post #MSWL—a manuscript wishlist—and you can reply directly to them if your manuscript fits their needs. Talk about access. I do think Twitter is better for professional connections rather than for readers, so it's probably not the social media outlet you want to start with if your goal is to find readers. However, if you are ready to pitch a manuscript or want an online writing community, Twitter is your place.

How to use Twitter. To build a following on Twitter, you have several avenues. The first is to start following people. Those with large follower-to-following ratios typically won't follow back, so choose one with a low ratio. Follow 100 or 200 people on a Saturday, and give them until Friday to follow back. Use https://unfollowerstats.com or www.manageflitter.com to find out who hasn't followed you, who hasn't tweeted in ages, and which accounts are bots that you might have accidentally followed. You can then decide which ones to unfollow. Then start over. Follow another 100 to 200 people. The idea is to keep the ratio close because, at 5,000 followers, Twitter won't let you go over with a large ratio discrepancy. Keep in mind both of these sites produce a ready-made tweet for you announcing you unfollowed so-and-so many people. Don't tweet that; it's just crass and amateur.

Another avenue to build a following is to start tweeting. I recommend three to five posts a day and not the same post. If you want to post the same link, use a different header or attention-getter. You have a maximum of 280 characters for each tweet, up from 140 a couple of years ago. Twitter is also previewing links with photos, making it look more like a Facebook feed.

Make sure to use hashtags to make it easier to get your tweets out there, but only use one to three hashtags. People want to be able to read the tweet and respond to it, and that gets difficult if it's littered with hashtags. (For a list of hashtags, see the Bonus Material #3: Hashtags section.)

My favorite way to use Twitter is to join live event conversations. It's an open conversation on something happening right now, and you can jump into the conversation at any time. You can find a lot of them simply by searching for the event, or look in the Trends column. I join these types of conversations, or threads, for writers' conferences, book festivals, and Alabama football games.

During the NFL draft, I followed the whole event on Twitter. Remember the Ellen photo from the Oscars that broke the internet a few years ago? That was because tweeters were live discussing the Oscars. In some ways, Twitter has brought back the joy of watching live television instead of DVRing it for later, but maybe that's just me. Either way, this is about a conversation, so jump in there.

A word about ads. You can buy ads on Twitter to increase your followership or click-through rate to your website, which will generate more followers. You can also buy ads to advertise a book launch or sale. In the drop-down menu under your profile picture, click on Twitter Ads. Click Create Campaign and decide which objective you're aiming for. From there, it's pretty intuitive. Again, the ad copy or the post you choose to use for the ad should be compelling and have a clear call to action.

Best practices. Like, comment on, and retweet posts you find interesting. Do this every day or every other day. Spend ten minutes and you'll see your following grow, because the goal is interaction. The more you interact and engage, the more you'll grow your community. Just remember, this isn't the place to constantly scream, "Buy my book." Well, no place is the place for that, but Twitter is about meeting new people and making new friends. You wouldn't ask someone you just met to buy your book, would you? Let them get to know you first. Answer questions in a particular hashtag. Ask your own questions. It's okay to put out that you have a new book every now and then, but not all the time.

Analytics. Twitter also has a great analytics section. You can see what types of impressions you made, how many profile visits you've had, and the growth in your followers. The audience data can really tell you a lot about your followers. The top interest of my followers is "dogs"—yes, dogs, and I haven't owned one in years. But the top lifestyle type is "online buyers," which really makes me happy since I want to sell books online. Mine this data to help you understand what your followers are interested in and how to reach them more effectively.

Pinterest

Compared to powerhouse Facebook, Pinterest is rather small, with only 250 million users (half of those users are located in the United States). However, it is the most popular social media site for women aged thirty to fifty-five, and even more telling and exciting for you as an author is that more than half of the millennial generation use Pinterest, men and women, and they use it as much as they use Instagram.

Those statistics alone make Pinterest a target for readers since the number of readers is calculated at 65% women. This is especially beneficial for writers of women's literature and any of the romance subgenres. It is also the fourth most-used social media site behind Facebook, YouTube, and Instagram, and those numbers are climbing. Pinterest also saw an increase in referral traffic of almost 30%. Lifestyle blogger Victoria Tiffany says most of her website traffic comes from Pinterest.

Pinterest attracts users in high-income brackets who are primed to purchase. More than 90% of its 250 million monthly pinners use Pinterest to find items to buy, and half of those say they bought a product after seeing a promoted pin. If you can harness their buying power for your book, you'll have a high likelihood of making a sale. If you don't have a book yet, then I recommend building a following on Pinterest so, when you're ready, you'll have an audience already familiar with you and your work. The average time spent on Pinterest by one user is fifteen minutes.

The top category on Pinterest is the Art, Supplies, and Hobbies category, unsurprisingly, but that category could be a gold mine for an author. And here's the clincher: The click-through rate (how many times a user clicks the pin to go to the website) is higher than on Facebook, Snapchat, or Twitter.

How to use Pinterest. To get started, create boards. Think of these like themed photo albums, or a visual file cabinet. One board should have a theme, and the pins on the board should reflect the theme. For instance, I created a board for the Pikes Peak Writers Conference and posted only photos from that conference. I also have one for the fictional town in my women's fiction series. It includes photos that remind me of the town.

Once you've created the board, it's time to populate it. That can be done either by repinning photos that are already on the platform, or you can pin your own photos. If you pin your own, make sure they include the URL for your website or blog. Pinterest drives an enormous amount of activity to websites and generally does that better than every other social media platform.

To build your following, create a board and start pinning blog posts, articles, or photos from your website. Similar to Twitter, you can repin, comment, or like posts from other followers and follow other pinners.

A Word about ads. You can also pay for ads, but, like Facebook requires a page, Pinterest requires a business account. It's easy enough to set one up or convert your personal account to a business one. You'll also want to install the Pinterest tag into the code on your website. All of this is spelled out intuitively so don't let it intimidate you. Pinterest runs a pay-per-click bidding system for ads. Find all this in the Pinterest Ads Manager. You simply select the pin you want to promote and bid on the target audience you're aiming for.

Best practices. Pinterest board ideas for writers include a board for your work-in-progress setting and other boards for your characters (their clothing selections, table settings, books she likes, any hobbies) and another board for book covers and blog posts. Always link back to your website or Amazon Page. Make sure to align your boards with the season. This helps drive searches to your boards. If you're posting to your blog or writing articles for your website, then make sure to use a "Pin it" button on the pics associated with those to optimize traffic to and from Pinterest. Finally, use good keywords because Google likes Pinterest, and good keywords will help your posts show up in Google searches.

Analytics. To use Pinterest Analytics, you'll need a business account. Then go to your settings drop-down menu and click on Analytics. What's great about Pinterest Analytics is you can attach your website and other social media accounts, and Pinterest can show you the type of traffic you're driving. This is especially good when you know what your ad objective is: book sales or followers. As with other data systems on social media, the information about your audience is available and gives you insight into who is digging your stuff.

Goodreads, Websites, and Email

Goodreads

Goodreads is another site I encourage you to at least have a cursory presence on, if for no other reason than it has a decent giveaway program you can use, and Goodreads was built specifically for readers. It's also owned by Amazon, so that at least makes it worth paying attention to.

As of the writing of this book, the site had eighty-five million users, and 60% of those use it monthly. Are those users just writers looking for readers, or are they really readers? There are two compelling statistics that bode well for writers. Eighty-seven million reviews have been posted since the site launched in January 2007. Just some quick math tells you that average is 7.2 million reviews every year, or 605,000 every month. That's a lot of reviews, and the data shows it isn't slowing down. That's a lot of reading going on. You could haggle over whether those reviews are for the same bestsellers or authors, but I think the basic takeaway is that the site has proven itself to be highly engaging for readers.

The second statistic is that more than twenty million books are added to Goodreads' Want to Read shelves every month. Again, I think it more than verifies Goodreads as a platform for readers and one to watch.

All of that being said, I don't encourage Goodreads as a primary marketing platform, simply because it doesn't have the reach of other outlets and in the late summer of 2019, they discontinued their ads platform.

While this outlet is a niche for readers and is steadily growing, authors have found it's still a work in progress. Goodreads reports the click-through rate for an ad is 0.05%. Compare that to 20%–25% for email marketing or 8% on Facebook. For the time being, I think it's better to use ad dollars on the big three and use Goodreads for their effective giveaway program (although there are other platforms for giveaways as well that are worth looking at: KingSumo, Gleam, and Rafflecopter).

When a reader enters your giveaway, Goodreads generates an automatic post to the entrant's Want to Read list and an update to their newsfeed. Goodreads also reminds the reader to rate and review the book after the giveaway ends. You do have to pay for the giveaway, and you are responsible for shipping the winners their books. If you're a KDP author with Kindle, you can do the giveaway with an ebook. Running the giveaway with advanced reader copies is a smart way to generate buzz prior to your book's release. Keep an eye on Goodreads because, while it's become a great spot for readers, it's losing ground as a platform for indie writers to find new readers.

Website

You absolutely must have your own website with your own domain. I do not get into website building or content in this book, because those topics totally warrant a book of their own, but I did want to mention it.

Your website is your little piece of the internet and belongs solely to you. It provides credibility to your online presence and, honestly, in this day and age, it's just expected. Readers expect to find your website. Event promoters want your bio and high-resolution photos for promotional materials and expect to find it on your website. News outlets and journalists will look for your website first for information about you. Publishers, editors, and agents will also look for your website to learn more about you. For those reasons alone, just create one, even if it's a static site that has an About You section and links to your Amazon Page or social media outlets.

A better reason to have your own author website is that everything on it is copyrighted, and that means all the information on it is yours. That is not the case with social media. While you do own those photos you posted on Facebook, they can use them however they want to. It's part of the user agreement. Same is true for snaps, tweets, or videos if you post them only to social media. Snapchat, Twitter, and YouTube can use those, and if the sites go down and they lose any of your content, you may never get it back. Awesome, right? No, and it's one of the reasons I wish they'd offer a paid service so I don't have to share ownership of my own content or risk losing it.

More importantly, posts you create for social media have the life-span of a gnat. The content on your website is much more accessible for the long haul.

I encourage you to start building a website now, if you haven't already. Set up a basic, static website that links to any social media sites you have and has a shop page for any books you are selling. That shop page should be a repository of all your books with links to the various platforms where readers can purchase the books. A list of icons with links to all your author pages at Amazon, Nook, Kobo, iBooks, or Google Play at the bottom of the main page works too. Not only is it more professional than simply redirecting to an Amazon listing, you maintain all creative license over all the content on your page, and your readers won't have to go anywhere else to learn about you and your books.

There are plenty of free, relatively easy-to-use sites to get you started: Weebly, WordPress, Wix, and Squarespace.

Email List

I do get into building your email list in this book (chapter 6), because, believe it or not, email is one of the most effective ways to reach potential book buyers. I can already see your eyes rolling. Numbers don't lie, my friend. I was astonished when I dug deep and looked at it. This is one of those tools I encourage you to start now. If you do nothing but gather emails until you have something to say or sell, it's worth setting up the ability to gather email addresses with an email service provider (ESP) like Mailchimp or MailerLite now.

Why Aren't People Working in the Afternoon?

When to post on social media is just as important as where and what to post. The analytics for each outlet should tell you when your followers are most engaged. However, if you want to skip this section, here's the nitty-gritty: **Post content during lunch and after work on weekdays, no matter which outlet you choose to post on.** Posting during that time will snag you some exposure and keep your social media outlet populated. This is a sensible first step for beginners and those who are not quite ready to start generating ads.

For those who are ready to step it up, this section discusses how to optimize your posts for maximum exposure. Each social media outlet has data to mine, helpful data to anyone trying to build a platform online. Analytics from those outlets indicate when users are engaging and responding on their platform. Just because the best time and day to post on Facebook is Wednesday at noon does not mean that's the best time to also post on Twitter.

Routinely, marketing firms conduct research into the analytics of social media posts and design a nifty infographic to depict the best times to post to social media. You can find the latest ones on Pinterest or with a quick Google search.

I like Pew Research, SproutSocial, and the Social Media Examiner for their latest research. Each of these puts out a study looking into the social media trends of the previous year. Twice a year, I look at the updated research and adjust my scheduled postings accordingly.

The following statistics are current as of the writing of this book and compiled from several different sources (also see www.jenniferlovettherbranson.com/SMforAuthorsResourcesForStudy for more information). However, pay attention to the analytics of your own content. That data will help you determine the best times and days to post.

Facebook

- The best times to post for interaction are Wednesday, noon and 2:00 p.m., and Thursday, 1:00 p.m. and 2:00 p.m.
- Decent times to post are weekdays between 10:00 a.m. and 3:00 p.m.
- The best day for user engagement is Friday.
- The worst day to post is Saturday.
- I'd also avoid posting in the evening and early mornings as they have the least engagement.

YouTube

- If you post during the week, post at lunchtime or after.
- Best days to post are Thursday and Friday.
- If you post during the weekend, do so before lunch.
- People spend more time binge-watching videos over the weekend.
- Worst day to post is Monday.

Instagram

- Best day to post on Instagram is Thursday.
- Lunchtime is the best time to post.
- Decent times to post are during the week between 9:00 a.m. and 6:00 p.m.
- Worst day to post on Instagram is Sunday.

Twitter

- Wednesdays and Thursdays are hands down the best day to post on Twitter.
- The best time is between 9:00 and 10:00 a.m.
- Decent times to post are everyday between 10:00 a.m. and noon.
- The worst day to post is Sunday unless there is a live event.

Pinterest

- Evenings after dinner is a peak time to post on Pinterest.
- Fridays and Saturdays are the best days to post.
- But any day in the afternoon is a decent time to post because views are numerous in the evening.
- Weekdays are the worst days to post.

Easy, for Pete's Sake, Make it Easy

This section discusses how to post your content using the Rule of Thirds. There are two rules. The first Rule of Thirds is how to get content for your site. The second rule explains what purpose your content should have.

The first Rule of Thirds details how to get your content out into the world:

- You can broadcast on social media or email.
- You can broadcast on someone else's media or email.
- You can pay for ads.

Broadcast on your outlets. This simply means post content on your Facebook Page, Twitter account, Instagram feed, Pinterest boards, or YouTube channels.

Broadcast on someone else's outlet. Make friends, meet influencers, and use their audiences to help push your content. Reciprocating email news is one avenue. You post a review or book from a friend, and they'll post yours. A blog tour is another route. You contact bloggers in your genre and ask them if you can guest blog. You can also post on your Instagram and have them post on theirs.

How do you do this? Well, honestly, there must be something in it for someone else. I don't mean that to sound icky or salesman-like. But if you approach someone else to broadcast content for you, have something to offer them. On my podcast, I ask for a sponsor for each episode. The requirement is to broadcast that podcast on the sponsor's social media outlets, email news, whatever they have. In return, I place a full ad about them and links to their books or social media on the podcast episode page.

Even if you have a small platform, you can offer to post for them: reviews, launches, speaking dates. If they feature you in their emails or newsletters, then return the favor.

Pay for ads. This third way of spreading your content requires you to first have an objective. What is the point of your ad? Is it to increase followership, increase the number of subscribers on your email, or sell a book?

Once you define your objective, you want to define your potential follower or reader. The reader is your target audience, and each of the platforms offers audience targeting for your ads. Learn how to target the right audience for each outlet and use keywords to create an ad that is worth your money.

Learning how to bid for ads and write actionable ad copy is something you'll want to spend some time doing. Unfortunately, that's a topic for a separate book and something you'll want to learn when you're ready. Suffice it to say, Facebook, Amazon, Google, and BookBub ads are probably the most important for writers.

If you're just starting out and have a book to sell, then it's time to learn how to use Amazon and BookBub ads. If you're building your platform and aren't selling just yet, then Facebook and Google are important. I recommend Facebook to start—use it to build your presence on Facebook and Instagram and to grow your email list. At this time, I think learning Facebook and Amazon ad marketing is absolutely vital when you're ready to sell books. The other advertising platforms can come after you've mastered those two.

The second Rule of Thirds sets the foundation for your social media feeds, and you're going to want to remember this: You don't have to create everything. Read that line again. You don't have to create everything. This Rule of Thirds says content comes from three places:

- A third of your content should be original.
- A third should be curated.
- A third should be user-generated.

That formula will help make life a lot easier on you.

Original content is what this book teaches you. Whether it's videos or photos or infographics, you'll want to spend one-third of your time creating that content. Otherwise, you're just an aggregator, and that's not compelling for readers.

Your content should be a way for the reader to get to know you. It can be as simple as a picture or as complicated as an hour-long podcast. Only a third of your material has to come from you. Blog posts, shout-outs, messages, trivia, pics, live video—you come up with it and you post it.

I write articles on marketing and I do an occasional podcast, so those constitute my original content posted to the Facebook Page. I also post photos of cool places I'm in or just whatever I'm doing that I think is fun.

Curated Content is the second third, which means the content should be curated from around the internet. What is that persona you're building? Is she a quilter? Subscribe to quilting society emails and pay attention to their blogs and videos. Post those regularly. Is your persona a criminal investigator? Then the news is your new best friend, because whatever crime you're writing, there is a story somewhere that would be along the same lines.

Because there are thousands of marketers online, I am always finding new and interesting blog posts, YouTube videos, or podcasts to post that I hope help writers with their own marketing. Curating from your favorite sites and authors is a savvy way to keep up your posts. It's also a good means of meeting other authors in your genre. Networking with those folks is beneficial when you want to cross-market later.

Another option on Facebook is video crossposting. If you produce videos, any site you grant crossposting permissions to can crosspost the video, and the analytics aggregate between the two. Collaborating with other authors' Facebook Pages helps you both and later can open additional marketing opportunities.

User-Generated Content is exactly that—material from your followers. Getting followers involved keeps you from having to come up with all the content. It also makes your social media community fun. Ask them to post videos or photos or GIFs (see chapter 5) of certain things: with your book, where they read, what they're doing right now, for example.

One way to get followers to participate is to ask about them. People love to talk about themselves. In my Facebook Group, Mondays and Thursdays are user-generated. Mondays in my group are always for goals—did they accomplish last week's goals, and what do they want to accomplish this week? It's an ideal tool for accountability. Thursdays, I always ask about their current work in progress and their writing process.

For your fiction, you can request input on your hobbies or those of your characters. Ask followers to show pics of them participating in the hobby you're discussing. Create a poll asking them to weigh in on character names or book covers. For nonfiction, ask your followers advice or tips on the subject you're writing.

Another way to find user-generated content is doing exactly that. Pay attention to the people who follow you. Watch their posts and, if anything resonates with you, repost it to your social media. This is especially helpful on Facebook or Twitter. Make sure to give the original poster a shout-out and credit for the great content. That alone lets people know you care about them and value their participation in your community.

Seriously, Give Me Back My Time!

Remember Platform Planning Sunday? It's the day of the week where I sit on the couch and schedule out all my social media posts for the next month or so. I use a scheduler to do it. The best way to keep track of your posts and make life easier on you is to use a tracker, planner, or online scheduler.

A scheduler is a dashboard of all your social media accounts. You link the social media accounts you want to use and create the posts there instead of in the social media outlet. It's like being on Facebook, Twitter, Instagram, and Pinterest at the same time. A content management app is a major time-saver. Once you finish creating the post, you'll have the option to schedule it out. Then you can view a calendar or list of all the posts you've created to see the outlook you've built.

If you're going to start with just Facebook, you don't need the dashboard. Facebook Groups and Pages have a feature that allows you to schedule posts up to sixty days out. If you're going to use Instagram, Twitter, Pinterest, or a combination of all of them, you really should use a dashboard.

I write down by hand on my content planner what type of post I want on a given day, and then I check them off after I load them up on the scheduler. I create posts three or four weeks out so if life gets in the way or I want to travel, the posts go up and I don't have to worry about it. I use Buffer and Facebook schedulers.

The dashboard also enables you to carry out daily maintenance—responses, retweets, comments—without having to log in to four separate accounts.

Types of schedulers—

- Hootsuite (was one of the most popular but is no longer free).
- Buffer (has become one of my favorites).
- TweetDeck (if you're focusing on Twitter, definitely a good choice).
- FB Scheduler (doesn't include the dashboard but is good if you only do Facebook).
- Sprout Social (paid service).
- BuzzSumo (paid service).

Then, make two hours on one day of the week your scheduling day. Mine is the first Sunday of the month. I spend a few minutes planning my digital content strategy for the week or month. Then I build all the posts for that month or the next quarter. This saves me tons of time later, because all I have to do is maintenance posts, commenting and liking and sharing for the remainder of the month.

Next, take another hour for research. Doesn't have to be the same day, but do this once a week or every other week. Research other writers in your genre. Do they have some posts you can share or comment on? Build that community with other writers. What types of information are they posting? Making sure you are a part of that professional community is just as important as building your own community. How do your posts compare to theirs?

Finally, spend twenty minutes or less every day or so in maintenance mode. Respond to comments or messages. Retweet other tweets. Like and share posts from others in your genre. This maintains the connection with your community and allows you to connect with other writers.

Analysis

I know all you English majors just got nauseous. I'm an English major, and the minute we start talking statistics, I run for the hills. But I've come to really appreciate analytics as a way of measuring how well social media posts perform. If you continue to truck along, posting without understanding if the content actually reaches anyone, you're wasting your time and probably not seeing good results.

The key to effective digital marketing is understanding the results. If you understand what's working—and what's not—then you can test and tweak your marketing efforts for better engagement.

All of the sites have built-in analytics, and, with a bit of time, you can understand them fairly easily. Just getting likes and followers isn't going to cut it. Once upon a time, a Twitter user could buy thousands of fans. The industry was impressed by that until everyone figured out the game.

More important, in my opinion, is to create organic, engaged followers. You want people who are actually interested in you and your books. The number of followers doesn't count as much as the interaction you have does.

To understand the quality of the community you're building, you need actual engagement with your posts: retweets, repins, comments, shares. That data really tells you if what you're doing works or not. Are your email numbers going up? Do you see an increase in engagement? What about sales? Do you see a steady incline?

Look at your posts. Which ones are doing well and which ones not so much? All the social media sites have really good insights and data to help you. The analytics can show you which day of the week and what time most people are interacting with your posts. Analytics can show you the demographics most engaged with your posts, and which posts are most active. You can tweak the types of posts you use and when you share them with this data.

I am well aware posts in my Facebook Group that ask for information about current works in progress garner the best interaction. I like these posts too because they tell me about the author or the book they're working on.

Once I asked for a GIF to show me how well their writing was going that week. It was clear some of them just needed a hug, so I posted a little bear giving a hug. This type of engagement and interaction is good for your brand because you are building community.

Community is exactly what you want to foster online—a place people can go to be distracted from their lives for a bit and feel part of something enjoyable. It's called social networking for a reason. When you do your analysis, you'll see what people are responding to and you can incorporate more of those techniques in your plan. These insights will also show you which types of content people respond to so you can incorporate that same content (or similar) into publicity for your book.

In other words, if you are getting a lot of engagement on video posts, a book trailer would be a great idea when you've launched your book or are offering a freebie or discount. If questions are working for you, then incorporate one that ends with buying your book. These types of posts should be sprinkled throughout your social media campaign but should not dominate it. If a spike in sales can be correlated to a particular post, then keep that in mind the next time you want to do a big push for your book.

On the other hand, be cautious about posting too many of the same kinds of posts because then you'll experience follower fatigue. You'll know it if you keep watching your analytics. Just tweak the frequency and you'll be fine.

If you want to use an independent source for your analytics, try out Socialbakers, Hootsuite, or Sprout Social.

YOU ASKED FOR IT... *Quick* TIPS

Pick one social media platform that works for you, and that's where you broadcast your content. Are you into pics? Then go with Instagram. Do you like vids? Rock on with YouTube. Are you about a little bit of everything? Facebook or Twitter. Are you into building photo albums? Go with Pinterest.

Although I started with Facebook, I love Twitter and Instagram. I'm still working on figuring out the best use of Pinterest for my specific vision, but I know it is one of the best places to drive traffic to my website. Bottom line: pick one and have fun.

Use the analytics to your advantage. They will tell you information that will help you create effective content. They'll also help you discover if you're targeting the right reader. Adjust as needed.

WRAP UP

- Pick a social media site that best fits your personality and objectives.
- Plan your posts.
- Use a scheduler to help decrease time on marketing.
- Use the Rule of Thirds when generating content.
- Analyze the data.
- Tweak your plan.

"The object of art is
to give life a shape."

—William Shakespeare

Yes, My Blooper Reel Just Went Viral

Everyone Gets an Oscar

Video is king on the internet! It is. Listen, I know we're writing books, but by 2020, 80% of consumer internet traffic will be video. It offers a behind-the-scenes, in-on-the-secret glimpse into you the author, and the world you're building. Video gives the reader a feeling of being in the "in" crowd," and that's how you're going to get readers talking about your next book. People click on videos because they want to laugh or be inspired. They want a break in their day. If you enjoy this type of content, definitely consider creating it.

If this isn't enough, check out these stats:

- Video is more likely to be watched than long pages of text read. Depressing for a writer, but that's comparing apples to oranges. What I'm talking about here is content posted on social media. Facebook is just one big scroll, and people will stop when a video is less than a minute long (thirty-six seconds or fewer is best), but they won't stop for a post with a ton of gray words.
- Video can increase your conversion rate and increase your traffic more than any other type of content.
- Use "video" in your email subject line and it increases the open rate by 13%. That doesn't sound like a lot, but when the average open rate for emails hovers around 20%, any increase is helpful. On a positive note, emails dealing with arts, entertainment, and publishing have an open rate of around 30%.
- Here's an awesome stat for anyone selling anything: 74% of consumers who watched a video explaining a product, then went out and bought it.
- Finally, and this is incredible, Google. If you have a video embedded on your website, Google is fifty-three times more likely to put you at the top of a search.

Readers buy books from people they know and trust. Videos are a fantastic avenue to help readers get to know and trust you. This chapter discusses live video, unedited video, and fully edited video. But let's start with this question:

What kinds of video should a writer produce?

- Conduct interviews with other authors.
- Interview a research source.

- Interview your own characters.
- Give tours of your writing space.
- Give tours of locations that remind you of your book's setting or are the actual settings, especially for nonfiction/memoir.
- Go behind the scenes of anything:
    - □ If you're a plotter, show how you plot.
    - □ If you're getting ready for an interview, broadcast that live.
    - □ If you're having drinks with writer friends, definitely do the video before the drinking starts.
- Host a Q&A session. Have a list ready to go beforehand and encourage viewers to contribute as you go along.
- Teach a course (not on writing, unless that is your platform. Use your expertise, one of your hobbies, or one of your characters').
- Ask for input on a cover.
- Are you holding a giveaway? Do it live.
- Read a chapter of your book.
- Share your favorite books (a reading list).
- Read a book review.
- Are you traveling for work? Definitely go live with some of that. (If you're on vacation, stay on vacation. You've earned that internet-free time!)
- Use the themes in your book. Is your main character a gardener? Good, then start giving live tours of gardens around your home that you love. Is he a police officer?

Attend the Citizens' Police Academy and go live each week of that.

- Share your own hobbies. Remember the talk about Alabama football. Whatever you're passionate about that isn't writing, use it.
- Check out Writers' Confessions, TED talks for writers, The Plot Whisperer, Chris Fox, and Orna Ross on YouTube.

Videos can be posted as seldom or as often as you want. The market is insatiable. Obviously, the more videos you have, the more likely you'll drive content to your social media page or website. That being said, keep an eye on Instagram and don't over-post videos just yet. As of the writing of this book, videos were growing, but photos still dominate the site.

When you think about how long your videos should be, it really depends on the content. If you create a weekly or even daily show, you could conceivably shoot for five minutes or less. If you're teaching, then you can go much longer. If you want to do a TED Talk-type of video, twenty minutes. If you're posting to Instagram, the platform only allows for one minute or less.

If you want to host a show, you could do these every once in a while, to boost traffic, or you could host a series on a consistent basis. I recommend either. To start, I would work with it once a week and see what you think. Not about results, because those won't come the first couple of times. But about how you feel about hosting them. If you enjoy the process, then move to a more consistent schedule.

If you want to create book trailers, make them less than thirty seconds long. These are like commercials for your book, and traditional commercial length is fifteen, twenty, thirty, or sixty seconds. The average length of a YouTube video is four minutes, but an ad is less than five seconds, so you need to get to the point quickly.

The bottom line is you can do videos about anything. Think about your public persona. What is that persona trying to build? Now build it visually. Find similar videos online and model the length and type from that research. The three types of video are live, unedited, and fully edited. Let's chat about each one.

3-2-1 Action!

Live video is exactly that—you talking to your readers, live, wherever you are.

Facebook will show your live Facebook video or live Instagram before it shows one of your other videos all day long. Makes sense as Facebook wants everyone to stay on their site, but they also make it super easy. The only caveat to Instagram Live is it disappears as soon as you stop live recording.

When you create a post, Facebook gives you the option to go live. Hit live, wait 3-2-1, and start talking. The longer you stay live, the more Facebook will shout that out to your followers so you'll gain more and more viewers. Same with Instagram. Just touch that TV-looking button on your profile, and there you go. Instagram will let your followers know. For Twitter, hit the tweet button and on the left side is the pic button. Press that and then hit live, you're all set. From the Chrome browser, go to YouTube and in the upper right corner, click on the camera and click ((o)) Go Live.

From YouTube: YouTube is slightly more complicated, only because its entire platform is about video. The exciting thing is that it gives you choices:

- **Mobile** lets you stream from the YouTube app on your smartphone, but only if you have at least 1,000 subscribers. The live feed is archived on your channel.
- **Webcam.** According to Google, using your desktop or laptop webcam is an easy way to go live. As of the writing of this book, the feature is only available on Chrome browsers.

Unedited Video

Unedited video is very similar to live video, but you are just not posting it immediately for whatever reason. Maybe you're at Yellowstone National Park, and you whip out your phone to take a video of a herd of bison running through your campground (true story for me!). But you can't upload it because there isn't strong Wi-Fi in a fifty-mile radius. Or you're walking through the National Aviation Museum, and the Air Force band magically appears as part of a flash mob. You don't want to run out your data, so you video it and upload it back at the hotel later. You get the point.

Best rule is if you're going to post your video on Facebook, Twitter, or Instagram, go less than sixty seconds. If you're headed to YouTube, then four minutes or fewer is good.

Look for opportunities everywhere. I don't care if you're grocery shopping, you can find an opportunity to shoot some video. Maybe it's your main character's favorite ice cream that you just found in the Kroger frozen food section. Awesome! Video yourself snagging some and tossing it in the basket. Maybe it's the killer's fantasy to eat bison and you just found some in the meat section. Grab the meat guy and ask him about bison and how it tastes compared to beef. Are you demonstrating a skill or teaching a class? Record it.

While I know this is supposed to be unedited video, it is a good idea to cut some of your video. Maybe you hesitate too long at the beginning. Maybe there is too much setup. Cut down the first ten seconds. There is a cut tool on your phone or tablet; use it. The best part of your video may be somewhere in the middle. Look for the scissors in your video editor to help you cut. This is also important because most people click out of videos in the first ten seconds. So if the video isn't getting to the action, you may lose viewers.

Film School Just Found a Natural

Fully edited video requires a learning curve and some software. As with anything, once you've played around with it for a bit and watched some of the instructional videos, you'll find it's easy to create video. Use the video tool on your smartphone or tablet for the easiest option to gather raw footage. You can use an app like VidLab to create and edit videos.

You can also use handheld and other types of cameras, then transfer the video from the SD card or through a USB cable or Bluetooth to your laptop. Either way, take the raw recording and open it in a software editing program. Edit, add music, subtitles, commentary, render, and post.

When you're editing, look at how quickly the video gets to the action. If it's taking too long, use the cut tool and make it shorter. Listen to the sound. The mixer will help you modulate the sound so it's more even across the video.

Add music. There is usually an insert key where you can underlay music to your video. Always use noncopyrighted music. The internet has plenty of it for free.

Always add subtitles. Subtitled videos get more engagement than others, and viewers watch longer. I think some of this has to do with accessibility but more likely, it's because viewers are in places where they can't listen to audio. If you're using Movie Maker, hit insert captions, and for iMovie, use titles because it doesn't actually have a "captions" button. In titles, there are several options, just use the option called Reveal Lower Third. In YouTube, you can use the automated subtitler or speech-to-text option, you can upload your own captions, or you can download YouTube's automation and edit it.

If you want to add commentary on top of the video, because maybe there is no sound in the video at all, you'll follow similar steps to subtitles. Each editor has a different way to add commentary or voice-over, but it's essentially adding an audio file to the video file. You can even use audio software like Audacity to create the file and then add it to the recording using the editor.

Types of Editors

YouTube is beta-testing their own internal editor in 2019, and, so far, I find it to be generally intuitive. If you don't want to deal with uploading a video file to an editor, then upload it to YouTube. You can just shoot the video on YouTube and edit in YouTube. However, since this is still in beta-testing, I recommend you use an already established editing platform.

Here are four editors I think will do the trick for you. They are the easiest to learn and use.

For Mac or PC

Blender
Lightworks

Mac Only

iMovie

PC Only

VSDC

There Are Weirder Ways to Learn

Are you interested in teaching a class or workshop? How about hosting a live book launch or book club discussion? Or just simply giving a presentation to your readers? Then start doing webinars. Most platforms offer the ability to interact by allowing questions to the host or a live chat. Live webinars can be recorded and posted on social media for later as well. It's a wonderful way to connect with your readers in a much closer or intimate platform.

The topic of the webinar should, again, do one of three things: educate, inform, or entertain. Think about the reader. What can you offer the reader?

While you can do this independently from social media with video webinar platforms like Zoom, Google Hangouts, Skype, Udemy, or Teachable, the idea here is to offer something to your followers on social media. To give more content and value to your video, include:

- Slides. Have slides to help augment the presentation.
- Recording. Amplify the recording when you're finished on other platforms.
- Chat. Live chatting is a way to bring readers into the discussion.
- Survey. Polls are important to gauge the audience and the effectiveness of the presentation.

YOU ASKED FOR IT... *Quick* TIPS

If you are in any way interested in video, start now. Learn all you can and get comfortable using the platforms. It is absolutely the most successful content on social media. Just remember that this is about you connecting with readers. The best way for a reader to get to know you is to meet you in person. The second-best way to do that is with video. Introduce yourself and start that relationship. I know it's a little intimidating, so here are some quick tips:

Start with private videos. What I mean by this is create videos for you and your close friends and family to start. Post the videos on private links and only share with the people you know will lift you up. This will increase your confidence, but it will also give you time to become proficient using the camera and editing software. You can even create live video on YouTube that is private.

Plan out your ideas. I know I'm saying "plan" a lot, but it is absolutely essential to building your platform. If you want to create videos, sit down and brainstorm all your ideas. Run them past people who support you. Narrow the list to types of content you are really excited about. Generate a schedule: daily, weekly, monthly, whatever. But generate it and stick with it.

Go big and go bold. Don't hold back. Make videos of anything and everything that gives you joy, and post those that help build your platform. The more you use it, the more comfortable you'll be with it.

WRAP UP

- Research the type of video you want to do.
- Model what's already out there in terms of style and format.
- Get the action going quickly.
- Go live often.
- Post regularly.
- Use subtitles in fully edited videos.

"I don't set trends. I just find out what they are and exploit them."

—Dick Clark

Hello, Is This Thing On?

Your Commute Just Got Tons More Fun

What would you do if you could have a half-hour of uninterrupted time with a potential reader? Tell them about your book? Talk about why you started writing? What about how you come up with your characters, story, or settings? What compelled you to write your memoir? How did you become an expert on your topic, whether it's the Civil War, cancer, or business leadership?

If you like audiobooks or podcasting, you are in luck. Half of audiobook listeners in the United States report they also listen to podcasts, so this audience seems to enjoy both platforms.

The US Census Bureau reports the average American commute time is 26.1 minutes. In addition, 70% of those commuters admit to listening to podcasts, audiobooks, or news during that time. My advice to you is this: fill that void.

But let's start with this question: Why do readers buy books? I know I've already said it, but according to everyone in the publishing industry (really, like everyone), books are bought because the reader knows the author. Now, to "know" someone doesn't necessarily mean you grew up with them and know their innermost secrets. It means you are familiar with them. Think about your favorite movie stars. You'll go see every movie Hugh Jackman makes because you liked the first one or two or three you saw him in. You "know" stars through their movies. You, like most readers, get to know authors in several ways:

- **You've already read an author's book.** You know if you've read one and liked it, you've read them all. C. J. Box's series on game warden Joe Pickett? Yep, I've read all nineteen in a row three times.
- **You saw them on television or YouTube.** Oprah, anyone?
- **You went to a reading.** I attended David Baldacci's signing at the Tyson's Corner Barnes & Noble outside of Washington, DC, for my birthday and am now an even bigger fan.
- **You've heard them on a radio interview or podcast.** I heard about ultrarunner superstar Scott Jurek on Rich Roll's podcast and now have read both of his books.

Radio's Making a Comeback, MTV!

The world is already primed to hold writers in high regard. If you can get a foot in the door, you can crash it open. For some perspective, think about this. The average YouTube video is 4 minutes 20 seconds, according to Mini Matters, and the average time a user watches a video posted to Instagram, Facebook, or Twitter is about 15 seconds. While these avenues can help the reader get to know you over time, think of them as the cocktail party. Podcast, on the other hand, is a weekend retreat. The average length of a podcast is 43 minutes 24 seconds. That's a significant amount of time to spend with someone.

The *Rich Roll Podcast* is, on average, ninety minutes. *The Joe Rogan Experience* is over two hours. The one I host, *Writer Nation*, averages about thirty-five minutes.

Another perk of podcasts is passive income. Additional income streams always help sustain a writer's career.

Four ways to utilize passive income streams with podcasting are:

- Affiliate marketing.
- Ads.
- Sell your own products.
- Sponsorship.

Affiliate marketing is where you promote a product and provide a link on your podcast page. If a reader goes to the site through your link, you'll receive a small finder's fee. Amazon is one of the largest affiliates, and you get credit for every item the reader purchases if it's part of the program, even if it's toilet paper, as long as they clicked on your Amazon link.

Ads on your website get a bad rap. I'm not a terribly big fan of having a lot of them, but you can allow Google Ads or other ads on your podcast page for passive income. They have become better over time, but just keep in mind, the more ads you have covering up your content, the more likely users will bounce from your site.

Sell your own products. Clearly, it's your podcast so you should mention your books. Books, giveaways, sales, all of it. But don't turn your podcast into a fifteen-minute ad of your work. If I can't start a podcast for ten to fifteen minutes because of ads, I won't listen to it.

Sponsorship. I'm a big fan of Patreon. Back in the olden times, when an artist wanted to make money, he depended on a wealthy patron to sponsor his art. This is a modern-day version of that. Patreon is a site that allows a listener to donate to your podcast simply because they like it. If you have ninety downloads on one podcast and each downloader pays $1 for that download, you've just made $90. I recommend offering Patreon status for your followers once you have a consistent podcast with consistent download numbers.

Now that you know why you should do a podcast, it's time to narrow down your topic to a niche. Maybe you already have one. *Writer Nation* is certainly not the first podcast to talk about writing and writers, but it is dedicated to writers telling their writing journey and the host talking about marketing. *Grammar Girl* podcasts focus purely on grammar. *The Writer Files* talks about the habits of famous authors. The *Story Grid* podcast discusses the structure of a book.

The point is that each of these podcasts deals with writing and the writing community, but they each feature a different aspect of it. Your podcast needs to have a sharp focus. What is it?

Podcasts exist to educate, inform, entertain, or inspire people, just like every other piece of digital content you produce. As you decide which one you want to host, think about its primary purpose. The *NPR Politics* podcast strives to inform about all things political in the United States. Rich Roll's podcast wants to educate and inspire listeners to be their best self. Each episode may talk about something different and unique, but the intention stays the same. You get the idea. What will your podcast do?

Here are some ideas for writers:

Educate

- Talk about a cause you champion (J. K. Rowling supports the Comic Relief charity to end poverty).
- Teach a skill or hobby you are into (Mary Kay Andrews is always talking about antiquing).
- Teach a skill or hobby your characters are into (Sylvia Plath, beekeeper, incorporated it into her stories).

Inform

- Talk about events: dates, conferences, workshops (your own appearances or events for your hobbies or causes).
- Discuss current issues: politics, Hollywood, education, military, literary news (Author Hank Phillipi Ryan, an investigative reporter and novelist, would be great at this).
- Give more details about your settings (*Crimetown*).

Entertain

- Read your book, a chapter at a time (author Kathryn Otoshi does this on YouTube).
- Discuss your writing process (*The Creative Penn*).
- Create a series (Smart Podcast, Trashy Books; Black Chick Lit; and MuggleCast).
- Interview fun people (*Kobo Writing Life*).

Inspire

- Interview motivating/inspirational people (*Stark Reflections on Writing and Publishing*).
- Tell the history behind your work (*Lore*).
- Give a motivational talk of the day (*Life Is a Marathon*).

Format

And how will your podcast educate, inform, entertain, and inspire? Format is important because your listener wants to know what to expect each time they download an episode. As with everything else about being an author, consistency is key. Your reader or listener comes to you because they have a particular expectation. What expectation will you create for your podcast listener?

Five types of podcast formats are:

Readings. Exactly what it sounds like. You read pieces of your work or someone else's you find compelling. Typically, it would be your book, and if you had a cohost or guest, you could discuss it. I think it would be fun to read your book and have your mom commenting on it as you are reading. But you can also carve a niche out of reading works related to your themes, messages, and characters rather than just your books. For example, my books are heavily influenced by my family's military service. I could read news articles about Medal of Honor recipients.

Reviews. A writer should be a reader. You could write book reviews and talk about them on your podcast. But you can review anything: movies, cars, magazines, items on Amazon. The thread throughout could be items your main characters love, current research on a medical condition for which you are an expert, or a movie based on your topic.

Interviews with guests. This is probably one of the easier formats, because you get to ask a lot of questions and let someone else do most of the talking.

Host only. This format requires you to think ahead about your topic. What do you want to chat about every week or every other week? This goes back to what you want to do with your podcast. If you're teaching, it could be a weekly "Ask the Teacher" type of format.

Conversations between hosts. Think *NPR Politics*. This is a round-table discussion about the topic of the week. It could be between you and one other person or a group of people, and the listener is simply listening to your conversation. *Story Grid* does this as the two hosts talk about how to make a book better. *Food Heals* has two hosts, and sometimes they interview someone or they simply talk about the latest information on vegan eating. *The Self Publishing Show* is hosted by New York Times bestseller Mark Dawson and newbie, aspiring author James Blatch. Those two talk about everything in the publishing world.

Get Started

You can hire out your editing and production or you can do it yourself. Production companies offer a wide range of services to help you. These companies can edit your audio, with professional mixing and mastering. They can create show notes, help you design cover art, upload to directories, and so much more. Most companies offer a tiered system, and if you're just starting out, the basic package is typically enough. Some examples are Podcast FastTrack, Podcast Motor, and Podigy. I have never used one and don't have an affiliation, but wanted to make sure you knew what to look for.

If you want to do it yourself, production can be done with minimal learning. If I can figure it out in less than a week, you can too. I watched a few YouTube tutorials and just played around with it. While it's no NPR-level production, my podcast is good enough to meet my objectives.

Here are the tools you need to get started:

Quiet space. I actually don't use a dedicated home studio, but that means I have to be really cognizant of noise. I normally do the podcast from my dining room table with my back to the wall. If for some reason I hear echoes or humming or road noise during a test run that day, then I go into our smallest bedroom where the sound is better. If you want to create a home studio, the easiest method is to put egg crate pads on the walls around your desk. Most of my interviews typically take place in hotel rooms when I'm at a conference or workshop, so the echo is pretty light. Listeners will forgive not having studio-perfect audio. But that doesn't mean you can set up in the kitchen where it will echo and pick up every little noise.

Microphone. Do not skimp on the microphone. It's the difference between amateur hour and a professional sounding podcast. I use a Blue Snowball Microphone. It's a middle-of-the-road, less than $100, good-for-beginners type. Make sure your microphone is multidirectional and can plug into a USB. If you're really fancy and want to record from your smartphone or iPhone, they have a microphone for that as well. Other microphone options are Blue Yeti, Rode Podcaster Mic, and Audio Technica mics.

Recording. You can do this on your laptop, tablet, phone, or handheld recording device. If you do long-distance interviewing over the internet, Zoom or Skype work well. You can use

Zencastr or ECAMM Call Recorder to record it. The audio file should be a .wav file you can import into the Audacity software.

Editing software. I use Audacity because it's free and has YouTube tutorials. If I can figure this out, anyone can! GarageBand is good too, but only available for Mac.

A word about editing: Some people take out all the "ums" and "uhs" and dead space. If it doesn't take away from the interview, I leave them in.

My format includes a sponsor note at the beginning, an introduction, the interview, and the end tag. That's it. Pretty simple. These are all individual files that I splice together using Audacity. I also underlay a music soundtrack on my introduction.

Music. If you want to toss some music under your introduction or at the beginning of your interview to spice it up a bit, there is plenty of free music on the internet. Make sure you use it. You don't want to be caught with copyrighted music. You can lay the music in as another track on your audio by using the directional tool to move it where you want. When I'm done underlaying the music (because it's the final step for me), I export the file as an MP3 and send it to my host.

Hosting platform. This is why audio is a bit more trouble than video. You can upload video files directly to social media sites like Facebook and YouTube. You can't do that with audio. You have to pay for a hosting service. I use Blubrry. Other options are Podbean, Libsyn, and SoundCloud. These platforms are basically the file cabinet storing my podcast file. Once they've stored it, the site provides me the URL for the file. That URL can be uploaded to any social media platform or website. I sync the Blubrry URL to my WordPress website using the Blubrry plug-in. It's super easy. You can also simply use the repository on your hosting site if you want to until you're ready to move it to your website.

Podcast art. Your podcast should have its own "book cover," if you will. A simple photo with the name and host is all you need. If you want to include a tag line (like a log line) and it will fit, do it. Flip through all the podcasts on iTunes to see what I mean. Once you've designed it, use a high-quality, hi-res graphic.

Webpage. While you can certainly use just your site on your hosting platform, I think it's important to use your own website. The repository on your hosting platform usually is much more functional than attractive. On your own website, you can create one repository for all your podcasts and drive readers to your little part of the internet. Each podcast should have its own page where you give details about the subject matter, any show notes and links you want to include, and any sponsor information.

Push sites. You'll want to make sure your podcast is on iTunes, Stitcher, and Podcast Addict to ensure a larger reach. Typically, podcasters wait until they have ten full episodes before adding to push sites. All of these sites are user-friendly and will walk you through how to upload to them.

Guests to interview. Easier than you think—I simply posted to a couple of boards I belong to and got a great response.

To Edit with Audacity

I recommend watching the few YouTube videos on how to use Audacity, but here's my quick tutorial.

- Once I record each section (or track) of my podcast—sponsor, intro, interview, end tag—I import each .wav or .mp3 track into the Audacity software.

- To cut dead space or any sounds out, I highlight the section with the Selection Tool (looks like an *I*) and hit delete. It's that easy to delete unwanted audio segments.
- To move each track into the order I want, I use the Time Shift Tool (looks like a double arrow ← →) and simply slide the tracks side to side until they are in the order I want them.
- To keep music under the audio, simply use the Time Shift Tool to slide it back and forth. If you want to lower or increase the sound, use the Envelope Tool (looks like an hourglass).
- When I'm done, I use the Normalization and Compressor tools (under the Effect menu), then Mix and Render (under Tracks), then export the file to my desktop folder as an .mp3. It's now ready to upload to my hosting platform.

I really enjoy podcasting, and have learned a lot over the past year. With just a little training and some equipment, you'll be set up in no time.

Just Read It to Me; I'm Busy

Audiobooks are hot right now for all the same reasons podcasts are. Simply stated, you should ensure each of your books is available as an audiobook as well. Readers won't necessarily get to know you on a deeper level like they will for a podcast, but they will get to know your voice. Yours literally, or yours in the book if you choose not to read it yourself. Either way, you are building a connection with a reader. If you're independently publishing, now is a good time to get into audio because a lot of traditional writers signed away their audio rights. They won't be flooding the market anytime soon.

You can fill that void. The trends confirm the explosion of readers listening to books. According to 2019 research data from The Infinite Dial by Edison Research and Triton Digital, 50% of Americans have listened to an audiobook. That's up six percentage points in a year. In addition, consumers of audiobooks admit to listening to more than six books a year on audio. The statistics also show that most people are listening at home, thanks probably to Amazon's Alexa. The Audio Publishers Association's (APA) research corroborated that 57% of the listening is done at home, while listening in the car was cited as the second-most-popular location.

The APA contends the United States was the biggest market for audiobooks in 2018 at $2.5 billion, and that's up $4 million from the previous year. Americans admitted to listening to an average of fifteen books a year, and a whopping 77% of those listeners agreed that audio helps them finish more books. This is a market just screaming for authors to jump in. Mystery, Thriller, Suspense is the top genre for audiobook consumers with Biography and Memoir running a close second.

According to Joanna Penn, *New York Times* and *USA Today* best-selling independent author-entrepreneur, "Audiobooks continue to be the fastest growing segment in publishing. There are some big technology developments in recent years that will continue to boost the growth of audio." She made audio a major focus for herself in 2019, and you can listen to several podcast interviews she did with professionals in the audio space on her podcast, *The Creative Penn.*

You can approach audiobooks in one of two ways. You can read the book yourself, or you can hire someone to do it for you. For fiction, I recommend hiring it out. I have a friend who trained specially to read fiction, and the training is intense. Unless you've had voice and theater training, and understand how to do different voices for characters, I caution you against reading your fiction. For nonfiction, if you are comfortable reading and teaching your work, then I recommend giving it a shot.

You'll want to use Audiobook Creation Exchange (ACX) because it distributes to Audible, Amazon, and iTunes. You have to have the book in ebook format on Amazon to upload your audio file to ACX. Findaway Voices is giving ACX a run for its money in this arena, so watch that as well.

To hire the audiobook production out:

- This really isn't a cheap endeavor. Hiring for an audiobook can cost anywhere from $500 to $2,000. Kindle recommends expecting $225 per every 10,000 words.
- Voices or Upwork or Fiverr are good sites to find professional narrators or voice actors.
- You can also do this directly with ACX.
- Write a proposal for the book and upload it onto the sites asking for a narrator. Generally, you'll hear back quickly with auditions and/or counteroffers. Make sure to include a timeline but make it realistic. Give a potential reader at least thirty days' notice. If you want to hire the sought-after narrators, you'll need to plan around the fact that it could take months for their schedules to open.
- Part of your proposal should include a payment plan. Some voice actors will take a cut from the sales of the book. Others want to be paid up front. If you have the budget, I recommend payment up front, because paying a percentage of the royalties could end up costing you more over time.
- Once you have the recording, you'll upload it to the exchange.

To do it yourself:

- First, go to acx.com and read through the submission requirements. This is extremely important because, more than likely, you'll end up using ACX to upload your audiobook and they are very particular about the product.
- Next, rehearsal time. Read the book out loud without recording and find places that trip you up. Either make a note to remind yourself about it or revise it.
- Plan for at least twelve to fifteen hours of reading time.
- The steps are exactly the same for audiobooks as they are for podcasting. Get a good microphone, find a super quiet place, and use editing software.
- Some tips for the best sound:
    - Record in a small room with a carpet (walk-in closets are fantastic).
    - Turn off anything that hums (refrigerators, furnaces, clocks).
    - Read from a digital device, not from paper (to cut down on noise).
    - Read a chapter from beginning to end.
    - Plan for a few days so you don't sound tired.
- Edit the recording. You can do this yourself with audio editing software (Audacity) or use an engineer. Find one on Fiverr or Upwork. For ACX, you can't upload the entire file unless it's less than 120 minutes. If your work is 10 hours, then you'll upload five files. Check out their requirements so you send what they ask for.

Final Steps (whether you or someone else recorded it):

- Upload to ACX, or an aggregator like Smashwords' Findaway Voices or Author's Republic. If you want it on Audible for Amazon or iTunes, ACX is the way to do it at the time of the writing of this book. For Amazon, they require that you verify the book you are uploading is also on Amazon as an ebook. The artwork must be square. Choose "World" rights because it offers 40% royalties for exclusivity. Non-exclusivity is at 25%.
- Market the book the same way you market your other work.

With the market exploding in audiobooks, it is simply not an area you can afford to ignore. It may take some initial investment, but I highly encourage every author to put their books into this format. I also encourage authors to keep an eye on this market. The industry is showing some initiative to compete with ACX, and better, more affordable options may be on the horizon.

YOU ASKED FOR IT... *Quick* TIPS

Even if you aren't wild about starting a podcast or convinced to turn all of your books into audiobooks, stay cognizant of this type of digital content. If you have a free minute when you're just surfing the internet or flipping through Netflix, watch one of the tutorials online. I predict a measurable explosion of audio formats over the next three to five years, and you'll be ready to implement if you start slowly working on it now.

For podcasts, start small. A simple, fifteen-minute audio introducing your characters is a nice way to work on your podcasting style and format. It will also help you learn to edit.

Develop your niche. This is vital. What can you offer that's different from others? Hint: your books will offer the same thing.

For audiobooks, start now. This is an investment, and I encourage it. You should see the return quickly.

WRAP UP

- Design a podcast for a niche.
- Podcast on a consistent basis.
- Use quality microphones.
- Learn how to record your own audiobooks or hire them out.
- Make sure to offer audiobooks for every book you sell.

"There are no rules for good photographs. There are only good photographs."

—Ansel Adams

A Trillion Photos (of Beaches and Feet)

I See Dead People

Do you like taking photos? How about putting captions on those photos? Then you're in luck! Visuals include photos and graphics, and social media posts with visuals are 45% more persuasive, encouraging much more engagement than any other content, aside from video. These types of posts are effective across all outlets, but Instagram and Pinterest focus solely on visual content.

If you're trying to reach upper-income women between the ages of thirty and fifty-five, and you enjoy photos and graphics, then Pinterest is your new favorite social media outlet. Photos about crafts and hobbies do very well on Pinterest. If you love being artsy with photos, then Instagram is your social media channel of choice. Use the filters and stickers to make it more fun.

According to Forbes, 65% of people are visual learners. Now, I know we're trying to reach readers, but we're also trying to build a community of readers, pulling them in to get to know you, the author, and to become part of your world. Remember the reader. If more of them are visual learners, then the best way to reach them is through visuals that teach them about you and your community.

Jeff Bullas, a *Forbes*-named top chief marketing officer, says 60% of consumers are more likely to buy a product that includes a visual. This also why your book cover is so important. Unfortunately, people do tend to judge a book by its cover, but that makes covers the ideal visual for your digital content.

As you're thinking about your photos, graphics, GIFs, and memes, think about your public persona and the community you're building. Best practices are to design your photo streams, albums, and boards around the themes and messages you're building. Create Pinterest boards with themes or motifs from your books: hobbies, locations, careers. Start looking at the world through the lenses of your public persona.

Does that mean you need to create a board or album with fifty photos? No. Start small. Just a few photos a week. You can work on increasing the number of photos, albums, or boards you post when you become more comfortable thinking about the world from the perspective of your camera.

I'm No Ansel Adams, But I Have a Smartphone

Photos are easy to post. You don't need an expensive Nikon camera. You can use your phone or tablet. Snap a pic wherever you are and use it. Anything and everything can be photographed and put on your feed, because you will experience something no one else experiences that day. Even if you find your subject mundane, someone else will find it to be interesting.

You can also use copyright-free photos. It is important that you use nonlicensed or licensed-for-reuse photos. For social media, lower resolution photos are good enough. For material a customer or reader might download, you'll want high-resolution photos. Your website should use a mix. Download speeds definitely slow with higher resolution, but for a main page or landing page—the page readers see first—make sure to use higher-quality photos.

For nonlicensed, licensed-for-reuse, or licensed-for-purchase photos, look here:

- Pixabay.
- Shutterstock.
- Google.
- Flickr.
- Creative Commons.
- Morguefile.

What types of photos? That answer goes back to what message are you trying to send. What are the themes and messages in your book? My favorite series is Nora Roberts's Three Sisters Island trilogy. Photos for social media to market those books would include coffee shops, gardens, bookstores, hiking trails, the ocean, and cool stuff you'd find in a mystical store. Susan Wiggs and Mary Kay Andrews stories usually are themed around family and small towns, so any photo representing life in a small beach town or in the Adirondacks would be good for them.

Where do you post? Simply think about the world you are building and use any photo that might reflect it. Once you find the photos you're looking for, post them on the social media outlet of your choice. Look for the photograph button or plus button and upload.

- Instagram: Use a filter to make it more fun.
- Pinterest: Build a board and post several.
- Facebook: Build an album or just post two or three at one time for best results.
- Twitter: No more than two per tweet.

Honey, Just Show Me

Graphics are another type of visual, and you don't have to have a Ph.D. in Photoshop to be able to create them. Believe it or not, I use PowerPoint. Yes, I am completely Photoshop illiterate, so I use what I know. Insert the pic, insert some words, save as a .jpg, crop, and post. That's good enough for me.

Graphics can be used to create all kinds of posts: memes, which are photos with words on them; GIFs, these can be several photos together or one short video clip; or push out a quote on Instagram, Facebook, or Twitter. For more readable blogs, or more easily digestible long posts, break them up with graphics. One of the best marketing tools for your website is a graphic on Pinterest that links to your website or blog.

To create graphics, here are three ways:

- Beginners use PowerPoint. That's me! Simply insert a photo and then a text box. Save the slide as a .jpg. Crop it using your PC or Mac photo editor. Then post it.
- Middle-of-the-roaders use Canva or PicMonkey. Both are intuitive tools to create graphics from scratch or an array of templates. It's an easy way to design using drag-and-drop features and layouts.
- Advanced use Adobe Photoshop. Photoshop is the blue-ribbon of graphics software, and there are plenty of tutorials to help you learn it. The nice part about Photoshop is the ability to layer and use transparent backgrounds.

What type of graphics?

- Infographics: These are the long visuals that have statistics or flowcharts on them. If you require that sort of data, use a reputable aggregator of data like Polling Report, Pew Research, and Statistica.
- Graphics of your setting: maps, demographic information, timelines, family trees.
- Graphics tell a story too: Writers can create graphics for anything. Statistics for your main character's skill or hobby. Ask yourself how many, how much, when is the best, what is the best. Fill in the blank, and that can be a graphic.

Where do you post? The same place you post photos, although Instagram best practices discourage excessive graphics.

Hipsters Do It, So I Definitely Won't

These images could fall under visuals or video, but because they are super easy, I put them here. There tends to be some disagreement about their definitions, but for our purposes, a GIF is an animated meme, and a meme is a static photo with words on it.

To add GIFs to Facebook or Twitter, you can use already generated GIFs by clicking on the GIF button and browsing through the repository. Just make sure you understand what message you want to send and what message the GIF is sending.

You can also create your own GIFs. These are less-than-five-second videos that capture some sort of human response to something. Use your smartphone and upload video to any number of websites like gifmaker.org, imgflip.com/gif-maker, or giphy.com/create/gifmaker. You can either upload your video to YouTube and provide the link or upload it directly to the social media site. Then follow the directions from there, and it's uploaded ready for use. As long as you have one to three seconds of video, you can create a GIF.

You can either post these yourself or ask for responses to questions using a GIF. This one has become lots of fun recently, because answering questions with GIFs can create some hilarious responses. Some questions you can ask include: Tell me in a GIF what you thought of my book, show me where you are reading my book, or which actor do you think should play my villain?

For memes, I use PowerPoint just like I do with graphics. I'll use either one of my own photos or a free one from the copyright-free repositories. Upload it to a PowerPoint slide and then insert a word box. Save as a .jpg and upload to social media. Easy peasy! You can also use Canva to create memes or use a meme generator like memegenerator.net. Again, upload the photo and follow the directions.

What types of memes? For memes, you can post quotes from your main characters or information about themes, history, messages, hobbies, or ideas from your book. Everything you think of can be used with a photo for your meme.

Where to post? Post GIFs and memes on just about every social media outlet out there except YouTube.

YOU ASKED FOR IT... *Quick* TIPS

The internet is visual, so you are definitely going to want to consider using visuals in your social media postings. Even if you do nothing but snap a photo with your phone and post it to start with, that's using digital content to your advantage. I recommend starting that way and moving to graphics, GIFs, and memes when you're ready.

Post what moves you. Until you're ready and comfortable posting often, simply post when you see something interesting. Start by training yourself to notice what's around you. Could what you see be in some way related to the world and platform you're building? Does that pizza place around the corner serve pineapple and kale pizza just like your main character likes? Great! Post it.

Don't worry about prettiness. Once you've trained yourself to start noticing the world around you in terms of your characters and public persona, simply post. Don't fret about filters or designs. Just post. When you're more confident and feel like you can do it without taking up a ton of your writing time, then work with the filters and designs.

Forget albums. Unless you are Annie Leibovitz or an Instagramming World Influencer, start slowly. Just post one or two pics a few times a week and leave it at that. You can work on doing more and creating albums or extensive Pinterest boards later on.

Have fun. Taking pictures is fun. It is. So enjoy your photos. Don't pressure yourself into perfection. Just have fun shooting and posting photos. You can work on themes and motifs and tropes later.

WRAP UP

- Use your phone to take photos.
- Use copyright-free photos from a repository such as Pixabay or Shutterbug.
- Create graphics using data from reputable aggregators, like Pew Research.
- Create graphics using Canva.
- Use a GIF or meme generator.
- Post photos a couple of times a week.
- If you're ready, create albums, boards, and streams.
- Design your streams from themes, motifs of your persona and world.

"Good friends, good books and a sleepy conscience: this is the ideal life."

—Mark Twain

The Peanut Gallery Needs Some Love Too

Little Bit of Everything in My Sights

Are you looking for any post that isn't a video, a pic, or a podcast? Have you run out of stuff to post? Are you exhausted trying to figure out what you need to put on your Facebook Page or Pinterest board? This section is designed to give you ideas for fun things to post on any of your social media outlets. Hodgepodged social media is just that: stuff you think of as fun and designed to help you boost engagement (shares, likes, and comments). Contests, giveaways, polls, email news, and reviews—you know, all the other stuff you post on social media. I also included 162 Ideas in the Bonus Material that adds to what we'll discuss here.

Between this section and the 162 Ideas, you should have enough pieces to build your digital content for the year. If you spend just a little bit of time filling out a social media planner or tracker (see Bonus Material), when it's time to post, you won't panic wondering what to post—you'll already know.

No matter what you choose to share, the content must make the follower think. Thinking gets your followers engaged, and engaged followers become readers, and engaged readers become fans who become super fans. Those people become your cheerleaders and tell all their friends about you. That's what we want to build—followers who bring in more followers.

How do you turn interest into fanaticism? Start by thinking about you, your books, reading in general, or anything related to messages or action in your books. The more engaging and fun you make it, the more comments, likes, shares, retweets, and, more importantly, interest you'll develop. In no way am I promising viral content. What I am promising is the ability to grow your community with compelling digital content posted at regular intervals. Just like all other types of content, every post should still educate, inform, entertain. If you can make it interactive and evoke emotion, you'll have a higher engagement rate.

The biggest point to remember is that while your posts can absolutely be related to your books, most of them shouldn't be. With the content we're chatting about here, you are trying to create a fun, relaxing place for people to be on the internet. Bombarding them with "buy my book" or "have you seen my book" posts won't keep them around. Use those every now and then. It's better to create community by subtly reminding people why they like you and what you offer, which is thinly veiled for what is in your book.

I highly recommend using a social media tracker or scheduler to create these posts out in advance as far as you can, then watch to see which ones work best for you. There are a planning guide and tracker in the Bonus Material.

I've found that people love posts that ask them about themselves and their work. They also like polls (because they're easy to respond to), giveaways (because who doesn't like free stuff), and games (because we all get bored or procrastinate).

If It's Free, They Will Come

For the sake of our discussion, we're going to put contests and giveaways in the same category.

First, design your contest:

- What do you want to give away?
- How are you going to get it to them?
- What do they need to do?
- How will you choose?
- How will you award the prize?
- How long will the contest run?
- When will you announce the winner?

Next, decide how you are going to logistically manage the contest/giveaway.

Use any social media outlet. This is the easiest way to run a contest or giveaway. Simply tell the reader what they need to know: when the contest runs, what they should post to win, when you'll announce a winner. You randomly select a winner. The easiest prize is one you can email. Think about that before you decide on prizes. Mail is a viable option, but it just requires a little more of your time.

Rafflecopter and Gleam contest/giveaway sites. Both of these have free accounts and can run your contest. Both are also relatively user-friendly. It does take some time to set up the contest, but they make you think through every part of your contest so you don't forget anything. Rafflecopter seems to be the most-used platform in the writing community, but Gleam is easy too.

What I like about using these, other than how easy it is, is the option to have contestants follow you on your social media platforms if they don't already. With enough traction, you should gain a few additional followers. With a paid account on Rafflecopter, you can also ask contestants to pin something on Pinterest or sign up for your email news.

Goodreads. Goodreads is basically Facebook for readers. In 2017, *Forbes* interviewed Goodreads's VP of communications who reported the site has over sixty million accounts around the world, and thirty thousand book reviews are posted every single day. In 2018, that number rose to eighty-seven million. If that's not enough to motivate you, more than seventeen million books are added to users' Want to Read shelves every month. That's a whole lot of potential readers!

I chose not to do a full-fledged chapter on Goodreads because, while the numbers are phenomenal, the reach and impact have not eclipsed the big five social media sites enough that I recommend focusing solely on it. That being said, if you have the time, I absolutely advise you to set up an author page, post your books, review other books, and engage in the forums. If you have enough books and are bringing in a significant monthly income from those, I advise you to engage in the Ask-the-Author feature.

As you're designing your contest or giveaway, make sure to also think about what you'll get out of it. Is it worth the money to pay for a service? If you have the budget, I suggest putting that money toward ads rather than contests. You can run contests for free on other outlets. The bottom line is that people love free stuff, so if you can run a contest once or twice a year, I recommend it.

Setting up a giveaway on Goodreads is easy, but you'll have to have a paper copy of your book and an ISBN. If you publish with KDP (Amazon), you can offer ebooks. Sign up for the Goodreads Author Program to get started. Complete a giveaway sign-up form, which is just as intuitive as Rafflecopter and Gleam.

Do the dates of your contest coincide with any major holidays that could pair well or would it be better to wait? Timing is always important for contests and giveaways. Think about when people are most likely to be paying attention. Sunday night in July? Probably not. They're too busy at the lake or shooting off fireworks. A Thursday night in December? Perfect. They're thinking about holiday shopping, and free stuff is appealing.

Once the contest ends, Goodreads selects a winner and sends you contact information so you can put the copy in the mail. This program used to be free, but as of the writing of this book, Goodreads switched to a pay system. Packages run from $119 to $599.

Didn't Work during the Election, Might Work Now

Polls are simply crowdsourcing ideas and don't have to be anything serious. They could simply be a "which do you like better" question about your book covers, laptop bags, character names, favorite whatever (color, travel destination, food, smartphone).

- Facebook and Twitter both offer a poll icon when you start a post. Click on that and go.
- For Instagram or Pinterest, use a graphic and ask for responses in the comments, or provide the URL as part of the graphic so when viewers click on it, they are redirected to the poll URL.
- For YouTube, create a quick video asking for responses in the comments.
- SurveyMonkey is a great tool for polls or surveys, and it's super easy to use. Sign up for a free account, and the system takes you through how to build a survey. I did my first one in less than ten minutes. You can post the link to any of your feeds or use it in email news.
- EasyPolls and SurveyPlanet are also good options for polls.

What to ask? Take a look at your book. What are your main characters doing, and where do they live? Mine are starting a new business and running for mayor at the same time in a small town in Tennessee. So, one poll could be five pictures of small-town squares to find out which one readers like best for the setting.

Another idea is to ask the name of the weirdest or funniest mom-pop restaurant they've ever been to. I like the Mason Jar and the

Grit. And one more could be to ask what followers call fizzy beverages where they live. Spoiler: I'm from Alabama. They are all cokes.

You can poll on whatever you want. Ask about favorite sports teams. If it's summer, what are their Fourth of July plans? Favorite vacation plans. Favorite winter storm activities. Favorite thing about __ season. Coke or Pepsi? Beyoncé or Rihanna?

The calendar in the Bonus Material includes a list of special and funny holidays to help you think about that.

Do You Ever Stop Nagging?

Anytime you can ask a question that is about the reader, you'll get interaction. This is different from polls because you are not providing possible answers. Think about when you've answered a question online. Did your favorite Instagram star ask what you take with you to the beach? How about your Twitter guru? Did he ask about favorite games? If it were an easy enough question to answer in fewer than five words, chances are you answered it. Your followers will be the same way.

Similar to polls, the questions don't have to be about writing or books, although working those in every so often is a good idea. Ask them anything. Similar to ask a question, try fill-in-the-blanks. People love those.

- What is your favorite ______? (book, movie, actor, restaurant, country, saying, person, historical moment, holiday, ice cream, Mexican food, city, way to travel, color, vacation spot, afternoon snack, Crayola color, smartphone app, TV show, thing to do at midnight, thing to do right after school, workout, outdoor activity, ride at Disney World, site to see in __ (city))

- What's the last item you grab before leaving for work?
- If money were not an issue, what would you spend $1 million on?
- If you only had $20, what would you buy with it?
- What would you tell your ten-year-old self?
- What advice would you give yourself at twenty?
- What is the one thing you can't let go of this week? (*NPR Politics Podcast, anyone?)*
- Would you rather have ____ or ____ for life?
- Would you rather meet ____ or ____?
- If you won the lottery, what's the first thing you buy?
- Name a food you refuse to eat.
- Give a movie quote that gives away the film without giving away the title ("You can't handle the truth!").

Use questions to also help you make decisions—book covers, logo designs, careers for your main characters. All of these are thoughtful questions for followers to know you value their input. In some cases, you can let them know they'll be featured in your next book if their idea was picked. Simple things like naming secondary or tertiary characters after them, or putting them in the acknowledgments section are easy ways to say thank you.

Party's Just Getting Started

If you really want to go all nerd, create a game to go with your book. I'm not talking video game developer level, although that would be cool. I'm talking about maybe a scavenger hunt or trivia game, tic-tac-toe or bingo, fill-in-the-blanks or anagrams.

Ask them to post the fifth photo on their phone or fill out a quiz you found on BuzzFeed and report the results. Quizzes are also something you can create on SurveyMonkey or OnlineQuizCreator.

Think about your book. If it's already published, encourage readers to find nine items in the book. If it isn't published, find six items in the book and ask readers to take pics of those things around the house. Those who post will be put in for a free prize.

You could also post a collage photo of four different pics and ask your followers which one they like best: book covers, briefcase for your main character, dresses for a ball, houses for your antagonist, or something not book related just to spark engagement—restaurants they like, favorite cities, favorite sports, favorite authors, favorite winter/summer activities. The possibilities for these photo collages are endless.

Winners can win free ebooks, gift cards, or grab bags, or an easy one like a shout-out from you on your next podcast or video or you can name a character after them in your next book. Get creative.

Come on, Storyteller, Give Me Something

You are a storyteller. So tell stories in your posts. They work because they are personal. I talk about funny conversations with my husband or my daughter. Family conversations can be hysterical.

One day I was eating lunch on the patio of a local restaurant, surrounded by a park with a waterfall. It was lovely. Out of the stillness, I overheard a family starting a game of "I hope I never get..." Each one talked about something. Dad said, "Arrested." Mom mentioned, "Pregnant." On it went. There were four children, and they just kept going as they waited for their food. As soon as the food arrived, the youngest boy shouted, "I hope I never get diarrhea!" I laughed so hard; I spit out my tea! When I posted that story to my Facebook Page, it generated the most engagement in a month. You can imagine the comments.

Now, this doesn't mean you have to eavesdrop to produce stories. Of course not. You're a storyteller. Draw from your personal life, your shopping life, your office life. Whatever you are comfortable sharing. Remember your public persona? Share stories that reflect that. These types of stories are generally ones readers or followers can relate to, which will garner active engagement.

Who Are Your Peeps?

Anytime you can post about your readers or followers is good. People love to be recognized. Develop criteria such as newest member this week or most active or random winner and simply thank them for following along and being part of the team. Posts like this encourage trust and community. They also increase your credibility with the community because you take the time to recognize them and show gratitude.

Ideas for shout-outs:

- Newest member of the group or page.
- Latest Patreon members.
- Happy birthday.
- Happy anniversary.
- New author.
- Author's new book.
- Latest review.

- Thanks for sharing your posts.
- Thanks for attending.
- Thanks for participating.

Opinions Are Like...uh, Never Mind

Reviews are actually one of the easiest posts you can write. You are a consumer and have an opinion, don't you? Then you can write reviews. You don't need a Ph.D. or years in the business to write what you think about a topic. I mean, if you do, that's a lot more credibility, but what I'm talking about is what your friends would talk to you about anyway.

Authors also do other stuff besides write, right? We read, watch movies or television, frequent museums, travel to new countries, eat dinner out, shop for clothes or sports gear, write at various coffee shops. Dave Ramsey, the renowned money manager guy from Nashville, says to look at your bank statement and you'll see what your priorities are.

Mine are definitely eating out, watching movies, and traveling. I write reviews about movies all the time. It's a nice creative outlet, and my family and friends tell me they enjoy them. I also love to eat out, so restaurant reviews are always fun. I'm low maintenance and love dives, so if the joint is a little dirty, I'm not gonna complain. I just care about the service and the flavor. So, what are your priorities? What are your hobbies? Make those what you write reviews about.

One word of caution. I'm not a fan of scathing negative reviews of creative content, especially books, since I'm a writer. It's important for artists/writers to support other artists/writers. If you don't like the book, I recommend you don't write a review. We aren't in competition with each other. What's nice about the reading community is that if someone likes one type of author, they want to read every other author in that genre.

It's also a small community, and building a network of supportive friends and colleagues means making choices about what you say about their work. Besides that, nobody wants to be around a Negative Nelly. Unless you can pull off funny reviews that at least give the benefit of the doubt to the owner and can find redeeming qualities, I suggest you don't write negative reviews.

For books, I have only written one negative review in my life, and I'm really not happy I did it. So, I now only write positive reviews or I don't write one at all. One thing I also do is only give four or five stars. A five-star book made me feel something. If I'm a blubbering mess or laughing out loud or scared to death, that book is getting a five-star review. If not, it's four stars. And that's not to say it was a bad book. It was a perfectly fine book, and one I enjoyed. It simply wasn't a knock-me-out-of-the-park-and-put-the-author-in-for-a-Pulitzer type of book. But I do think the author deserves the boost a review can give. I know how hard writing is, and I want to make sure everyone knows what I loved about their book. Specific information about what makes the book significant is important in the book review.

Now, negative reviews about movies, hotels, or restaurants or an experience you had? Okay, we can talk. First, make sure you weren't just having a bad day. Second, will the review actually help people or make you feel better? If it's to help people, then go for it. If you're just being a jackhole because someone was mean to you, think twice. But simply pointing out what didn't work for you is good because you're probably a typical viewer or customer.

My rating for movie reviews is whether it's worth a trip to the actual movie theater or a Netflix night on the couch. If it's worth the trip, should it be a Saturday night or Sunday matinee? My favorite movie of 2018 was *Paddington,* and it garnered a Saturday night with large popcorn and dinner afterward for discussion kind of rating. Make sure you talk about the acting, directing, storyline, and what you loved or didn't about it. If you aren't sure who some of the actors are, use Rotten Tomatoes or IMDB to help you.

For restaurants, I review what I loved and didn't, and a suggestion to fix it. In Korea, the Mexican restaurants never bring you more than a quarter cup of salsa (don't ask, I have no idea why) unless you ask for more. Even then it's usually less than the original teaspoonful. Sigh. I'm always telling the owner that if they want to appeal to Americans, they really should understand our salsa intake and offer a bowl more similar to a trough than a teaspoon.

In the United States, I compliment the service if it's good. I don't mention it if it's middling. But if it's rude, I will mention it. If a server wipes the table crumbs all over my daughter and then walks off (true story), I'm going to write a review suggesting they fire that girl. Not really, but I did discuss the rudeness of the server, and I included how well I liked their food because we did. The flavor of the food is super important to me too. If it makes me happy in the first bite, it's a keeper. I don't really notice portion sizes unless I'm still hungry when I'm done, which, frankly, is hard to do in the United States.

So, think about what you want to review. Develop your own rating system (stars, noses, attagirls, whatever) and let the folks know what you think. Always offer positive feedback and suggestions for fixes if you can.

Old School Is the New School

If you do nothing else with your marketing besides maintaining a website, I absolutely advise you to build an email list. Yes, I know this isn't about social media posts, but I think it's important to include here because you'll use your social media to publicize your list and grow it.

Back in the day, I would have told you it was nuts to depend on email. It was going out of style. It was fading to instant messaging and social media platforms. Email was antiquated. Well, I take it back. Email is also resilient. While social media sites come and go, even the influence and reach of Facebook and Twitter ebb and flow. For the foreseeable future, email remains the most effective way to reach an audience—an audience that wants to hear from you. To drive home this point, check out these stats:

- According to Forrester Analytics, email usage is actually growing, including those aged 12-17, which saw a jump from 69% to 82% from 2014 to 2017 *("You've Still Got Mail," January 2019 Forrester blog post by Brandon Verblow).*
- A full 71% of respondents to the ExactTarget's Global Research poll admitted that email is the first thing they check when they wake up in the morning.
- Additionally, 91% of US customers (people who are online to buy stuff) use email daily.
- If you can believe it, email is six times more likely to get a click-through than a tweet.
- Research across the marketing world has shown that email marketing for Black Friday deals are extremely effective and, in some cases, have shown to be more effective than social media posts. This makes sense because people are primed to buy and looking for deals during that time.

> (Romance writers the world over report better sales on Christmas holiday books than at any other time of the year.)

While Facebook may be taking over the world at more than 2 billion users, the number of email users worldwide is projected to reach 3 billion by the end of 2020. You may not be putting books out in Thailand yet, but you may one day. Knowing email stats and effective email strategies will even help you reach an audience in Bangkok.

Okay, so now that you know people still read emails, why is it better than social media?

Two things: content and users. Facebook owns everything you put on it. Instagram, Twitter, Snapchat—all own the content you post. Well, they at least own the platforms you've put that content on and have shareable rights to your content. In contrast, whatever you write in an email is yours, forever. Ownership is important. It can't be taken away or exploited for someone else's use.

Guess what else social media outlets own? The users. This is probably the most important takeaway for you. When you build an email list, that is yours. You own it, and you can move it from platform to platform, never losing it. In addition, and arguably, more importantly, that list is a group of readers who gave you permission to talk to them, directly to them. You don't need an ad boost or to be a guru in social media algorithms to talk to them. You can email them directly. They know who you are and what you are offering, which makes them more likely to be readers of your work and likely buyers of your books.

Another note: click-through rates. A click-through is when one of your readers clicks on the link you provided in your email news. Email consistently drives higher click-through rates to your website than social media. Who doesn't want more people to visit their website?

Last item: relationship building. An email is a direct note to your reader. Yes, social media is this too, but it's more of a wide net rather than a captured audience. If you aren't paying for ads on your Facebook Page, your reach or posts-seen rate is less than 5%, even less on Twitter. Email delivery rates hover around 75%. (The remaining 25% end up in spam for various reasons. We'll talk workarounds.)

But these rates mean you are guaranteed to have your information in front of 70% more followers on your email than you will on any social media outlet. Once the email is delivered, it's on you to have written content compelling enough to engage your reader.

Build Your List

I'm hoping if you're at this section, you're convinced you need an email list. Before we get into it, however, I'd like to dispel the notion that this is a quick process. It isn't. It takes time, but building relationships in all settings takes time.

Think about this: Even if your list is twenty-five people, those twenty-five people asked to be included in your world and know what's going on with you. Think of them as twenty-five people who showed up at your party because there is something you're doing they like. So, make it worth their while. Over time, that list will grow and you'll have hundreds or thousands of people who want to get in on the action.

First things first: Set up your provider and link, so people know where to go to sign up for your news.

1. Pick an email service provider (ESP). I use Mailchimp because it's free for the first 2,000 subscribers and relatively easy to learn. Others are MailerLite, ConvertKit, ConstantContact, Mad Mimi, and AWeber. I recommend Mailchimp for beginners because it is intuitive and has templates, A/B testing, and decent analytics. Mailchimp also offers enough automation to get you started. In May 2019, Mailchimp overhauled its platform and a lot of writers jumped to MailerLite. It also offers templates, A/B testing, and decent analytics as well as automation. There are some quirks Mailchimp users will work through, and it's free for only the first 1,000 subscribers, but it's a good alternative to Mailchimp.

For those who are already efficient at email news, I recommend ConvertKit because it makes segmenting your list (sending different emails to different groups of people) super easy. If you are selling multiple products, teaching, and trying to reach different customers at separate intervals, this is definitely for you.

2. Create a compelling landing page. This is key. The landing page is your first impression. It can be created on your website, or you can design it with your email service provider. It's your elevator pitch. It's where potential readers decide to stick with you or not. So, tell them who you are, what you offer, and what they'll get out of signing up with you. It's a good place to let them know how often you'll send emails and reassure them you'll never sell their email or send spam.

3. Offer a freebie for signing up. A sure-fire way to build your list is to promise free stuff. I mean, who doesn't like free stuff? It doesn't have to be complicated or a huge file. I offer a free book, but there are tons of ideas: access to a closed Facebook Group, the first couple of chapters of your book, behind the scenes of where you write, bits of your research, maps, family trees, recipes, best-of lists. Be creative. Spy thrillers can provide redacted case files. Romance writers can offer Valentine kits. Fantasy writers? Maps of their worlds. Memoirists can provide family photos. Historians can offer vintage photos and background documents or unpublished interviews. Business books authors can provide checklists and assessment tools. Free first-in-a-series books are the easiest and most successful if you have a series. Bottom line is to offer the incentive to sign up for your news.

4. Enable double opt-in. This is important because of antispam laws. Have you wondered why almost every newsletter or email subscription you sign up for requests you to confirm your subscription? It's because the law is designed to keep charlatans from jamming up your inbox with unwanted email solicitations. If you want to know what constitutes spam, check out your spam box. You can always snag a cool million if you want to offer your bank information to the Nigerian prince or buy drugs for your sexual problems or get an ego boost from all the lonely people out there looking to make friends. Most of these are phishing attempts, scams, and other nefarious ploys to rob you blind. By requesting confirmation to be on your list, you are protecting your reader from exploitation and protecting yourself from litigation.

Next, after you've set up your provider, you need to broadcast that sucker everywhere:

- If you already have books on the market, put the sign-up link in the back matter.
- Add a big, hard-to-miss sign-up link or pop-up on your website.
- Put an unobtrusive sign-up link on every page of your website.

- Use the "learn more" button on your Facebook Page. (Not the "sign up" one because it turns people off).
- Pin a tweet to the top of your Twitter Page.
- Pin a post at the top of your Facebook Group.
- Post to your Facebook Profile, Group, and Page.
- Tweet it to your Twitter followers.
- Add a link on your YouTube channel, Instagram, and Pinterest profiles.
- Boost the Facebook post on your Page.
- Amplify a tweet with a small ad buy.
- Include the link in your email signature block.
- Put the link on any paper materials you take to conferences and retreats.

One note on building your list: I do not encourage buying emails. There are few exceptions to this. You want to build a list of people who want to hear from you and have told you they want to hear from you. The relationship will be stronger because of it. The only exception to this is list builders out there that specifically exist for readers to be included in an author's email list. If you use these, make sure you fit the description of the list. In other words, if you're a thriller writer, don't buy a romance list. Good way to hemorrhage users.

Last note on this. Some authors build their lists by inviting everyone in their email contact list. I have 500 folks in mine, and they range from an old aunt I haven't seen since I was six to a colleague who hates reading, so I put this idea in the same category as buying emails. Proceed with caution. Does your boss from five jobs ago really want to read your fiction? Does your aunt? Think of this like Facebook Groups. Has anyone ever "invited" you to a group, which used to mean "added you"? Did you ask to be added? Did they ask you if you want to be added? Same concept applies to your personal contact list.

Send Your Email News

So, what do you email people? Whether you send a newsletter, email message, or short email news, the information included needs to be beneficial to the reader.

First thing I recommend is to not call it a newsletter. The market is saturated. Call it something like, "VIP Access to Super Cool Content," or something close. Whatever you choose to send, the email is not about you. I mean, it is, but it's not a platform for your manifesto or weekly download of activities. It's about what you offer the reader. Keep that in mind every time you write your email.

One suggestion I recommend to start is to scroll through all the newsletters you subscribe to. What do you like about them? What do you hate? Generate a list of ideas and go from there.

Because email marketing has become quite the thing of late for authors, we really need to talk about obnoxious. No matter which platform you decide to market on, if you are obnoxious, you'll fail. Remember when Twitter was all the rage and newbies were constantly posting links to their books? That is obnoxious. And it doesn't work. Same is true with email. You are not emailing readers to become their best friends or to bombard them with requests to buy your book. You are emailing them because they gave you permission to tell them about yourself and your fiction. That's it. Make it interesting and fun and something they look forward to.

And use A/B testing to help you. Use the same subject lines but different formatting or information to see which one gets the better click-through rate. If it's a similar rate, try different subject lines and see which works. This information will help you continually meet your subscribers' demands and, hopefully, get you more clicks to sell.

Here are some content ideas for your email to get you started:

- Progress reports on the current work in progress.
- Book launch announcements.
- Events and appearances.
- New blog posts.
- Research.
- Photos of your last trip and what you learned (keep the size small so you don't clog up their email box).
- Positive reviews your book received.
- Interviews with research subjects or other authors.
- List of your favorites (books, authors, movies, plays, music).
- Promotions and/or giveaways.
- Deleted scenes (also good for a freebie).
- Milestone news (anniversaries, birthdays).
- Backstory (you know, all that stuff you wanted to put in your book but your agent made you take it all out).
- Quotes and questions.
- Call to action (attend the event, meet the author, sign up for a giveaway, follow on social media, book buy links at the bottom in regular font).

Pay attention to your subject line. This will determine if someone opens your email or not. I can't say enough about this. The more you make the content about the reader, the better the odds of them opening your email. Think about it like the ending of a chapter. You want the cliffhanger. You want them to turn the page. A subject line is exactly that. What it isn't is Click Bait. You must deliver on whatever promise you offer.

Brainstorm twenty-five different headlines using snark, humor, emotion, directness. Use that list to find your best one. This is also where A/B split testing comes in handy. Use two of your subject lines and see which one gets more opens.

- Ask a question (Did you know? What if? Are you?).
- Create a sense of urgency (The time is now for ___. Today only. Changes are coming!).
- Talk directly to the recipient (use "you").
- Use punctuation like exclamation points or emojis.
- Promise something (I've got ___, or You'll want to see ___).
- Do you know where to ___ right now?
- Did you know we have ___ in common?
- A 5-step plan to help you ___.
- Ask the subscribers what they are looking for. Give them a survey.

Best Practices

Set up an auto-email train. An email train, drip campaign, or automation campaign is a set of emails you send to new subscribers. Start with a welcome email that is sent as soon as a new subscriber joins your list. Introduce yourself and tell them what they can expect. Provide a link to your freebie. A week later, send another email with interesting facts and information about you, your books, and your characters or for nonfiction, your research and background. I've seen some introduction email trains of five emails and some of twelve. I send six, and the first one includes the freebie. The last one includes another freebie.

For a fiction author, I recommend three, and then monthly until you are comfortable and achieving high open rates. For nonfiction, I recommend up to six, and then again, monthly or biweekly. Whatever you do, do not send email every day, and do not make your auto-sequence a set of request emails. These should have evergreen content to help the reader get to know you and your fiction.

Believe it or not, people really don't care how many emails you send them. When I first heard this, I was floored. No way! Don't we get way too much email? But studies show they just stay on lists. This will be a problem when you start paying for yours, but until then, don't sweat it. When it does become a problem, you can send a "Hey are you still interested?" email and if they aren't, or don't respond, then you can boot them from your list. It's important to have people on the list who want to be there.

Segment your email lists. By doing this, you will know who your fans are and who might need a little more coaxing. If you know one subscriber opens everything, then send them emails for more cool stuff by you. If they don't open at all, ask them if they still want to receive your emails and explain, in a nice and cheery manner, that they'll be unsubscribed if there's no response. I've seen this done in a number of ways that aren't off-putting or rude. This is super important when you start paying for subscribers.

Set up multiple landing pages. For each place you broadcast your email sign-up, create a landing page. This helps you determine where people are signing up from. This is helpful if you want to buy ads on a platform because it's performing better than others. Setting up the landing pages is pretty basic on any of the email service providers.

Try A/B split testing. Most email providers offer this, and it's a way to see which email subject line or content gets more response. Usually, you want to have a large list (at least 250 with a decent conversion rate – 30% or more) before using this because you'll want a large pool of respondents. The idea is to split your list in half and send each half the same email but with different subject lines to test which one gets a higher open rate. Or use the same subject line but different content or a different format to determine which one of those gets more click-throughs.

Be careful of spam words. *Free, credit card, guarantee, money back, 100%, price, cost.* These are words that get your email sent straight to spam. Avoid them at all costs. There is a link on my website with a comprehensive list of words to avoid. Click www.jenniferlovettherbranson.com/SMforAuthorsResources.

Treat the people on your list like rock star visitors to your VIP club. Include something for subscribers only, an item people can't find on your website or social media platforms. Some writers offer extra chapters or character interviews or even extra podcast episodes.

Be relatable. Think of this as a conversation with your best friend about what you're up to these days. If it sounds like a stiff, hard-selling tactic, readers will bolt. If the email sounds like an endless string of questions they should answer, they'll also bolt. Simply write a nice note like you would to any friend and let them know what's up with you.

Use analytics and continually tweak. Just like with A/B testing, use the analytics to your advantage. Who is opening all of your emails?

Those might be your super fans. Who is clicking on what? Those also might be your super fans. Who is opening but not clicking? They might need a nudge. Who is clicking but not buying? Another nudge. This is why segmenting the list is important.

YOU ASKED FOR IT... *Quick* TIPS

This section has a lot of information and tons of examples, and that's what I want you to think of this section as—a giant list of ideas for you to consider. You certainly do not need to use all these ideas, except maybe the email list. Use this section as you brainstorm the types of posts you want to include in your tracker or scheduler.

Pick one or two. If there is something in this section that looks fun to you, put it on your list and try it out. I do recommend mixing it up. So, don't do a fill-in-the-blank every day. Do that one day and use a question the next. It's a similar type of post and won't require you to branch out too much. When you're ready, add other types in there.

Mix and match. When you're comfortable using different types of posts, brainstorm from the ideas in this section and use a different one every day. This will keep the online community interesting and fun, and keep your followers excited to come back for more.

Don't wear out the follower. If you like to use interactive posts, great! But don't wear out your followers. I typically only post two of those per week. The rest of the week, I post information to inform or entertain.

WRAP UP

- Interactive posts will garner the most engagement. Use a couple of times a week on each outlet.
- Tell a funny story once a week.
- Do a giveaway every so often. Even if you haven't published, give away a gift card.
- Shout out to your fans. They'll love you for it!
- Start building your email list now.
- Use Mailchimp or MailerLite to build your email list. MC is free up to 2,000 subscribers. ML is free up to 1,000 subscribers.

"No one is useless in this world who lightens the burdens of another."

—Charles Dickens

Keep at It; You're Not Done Yet

Charles Dickens is right. You are not writing for yourself. You're writing for your reader. Be proud of that. Bringing art, creativity, or answered questions to another human being is a fantastic way to live your life. It's incredibly fruitful and fulfilling. I hope what you learned in my book is how to build a solid following without wasting your time, and how to get your book in the hands of your reader.

This section wraps everything up. This book was developed to help you think through the types of social media outlets available and the types of posts you can use to grow your readership. To do this effectively, understand who your reader is and decide what you want to offer that reader. To do it efficiently, plan everything and set aside one day a month to schedule your posts. Then do maintenance posts for twenty minutes a day. That's the big secret. **Plan. Schedule. Maintain.**

To make this work for you, below are my essential recommendations:

- Design your public persona and decide what you're comfortable sharing.
- Develop your marketing plan.
- Brainstorm your digital content on a tracker.
- Utilize a dashboard to save time.
- Start with one or two social media outlets.
- Start with two types of content: videos, audio or visuals, and one from the hodgepodge section.
- Keep learning. Try new things and see which ones you gravitate toward.
- If you love it, your followers/readers will too.
- Always remember the reader. Whatever you post should benefit them.
- Interactive posts yield high engagement, and videos yield high impressions.
- Don't be overwhelmed. You do not have to do everything.
- Write a good book. This comes first. Don't sacrifice the book for the marketing.

By no means is this all you need to do for marketing, but it gets you off to a good start.

The remainder of this section contains the Bonus Material. This material gives you a roadmap to get started.

- **The Social Media Planning Guide** helps you brainstorm and create the platform.
- **The Tracker** helps you plan out your posts. The posts on the tracker can be scheduled out on a dashboard and exported to an Excel spreadsheet so you can track your results. Those results will help you tweak your posts.
- **162 Ideas for Digital Content Posts** are ideas that can be used exactly as they are. You simply plug them into your scheduler. You can tweak them with your own themes and messages to make them your own.
- **Hashtags** are key on Instagram and Twitter. I included a list of 162 hashtags to get you started. Some are genre-specific, and others are on writing or communities. You should be able to find several to fit your particular needs.
- **Holidays** are a fabulous way to centralize your posting and give you brainstorm ideas for that particular day. For instance, on National Donut Day, you can ask your followers to post all things circles, or if you write thrillers, mention cops in the donut shop. You get the idea. There are over 400 holidays listed out for you.

Take all these tools and make it easy on yourself. Plan out your platform as far out as you can, and give yourself time back in your day. I know I've said it a million times, but take one day a month and schedule the posts you just spent all that time planning, then you'll only need to do maintenance posts every day or every other day. Follow this formula and you will build a following. It will be slow, but don't let that discourage you. Stick with it, because you need a foundation when you get ready to actually publish the book or if you want to boost sales.

The focus of this book is to get you started. Create a space for your readers. That's essential. You will grow slowly, but remember, this is a marathon, not a sprint, and those people wouldn't follow you if they didn't like what you were giving them. Even if you only have 25 followers, use that to your advantage when it comes time for the book launch. I once heard a writer refer to those few people as the ones in your cool clique. They signed up to be with you, so give them something to talk about. When the book is launched, they'll be the ones to buy it and tell their friends about it.

If you already have books out, then continue to grow your following by posting often and being available. Your social media should expand to more content. Not necessarily to more outlets. If you already post funny photos, then start posting funny videos. It's about increased, engaging content, not extending yourself. This content should drive your followers to talk about you. Again, plan these out and use a scheduler so you don't have to do this every day.

In addition to social media, for new authors or those wanting to boost their marketing, I recommend building a website, even if it's a static one with an About You section and links to your social media. If you'd like to expand it, your website should include an events section so readers will know where you'll be. It should also include a page with all your books and a page with some photos and videos about you and your work. This increases the ability for Google to find you.

Your email list should grow. If you haven't been actually sending emails yet, now's the time. But remember, no one wants to be pitched to on the first date. Let them get to know you before you ask them to buy anything. I recommend at least one email a month if you're just starting out. Two if you have books to sell. Make sure the content is compelling. Stick with your public persona and provide tidbits about your life based on that persona. Be careful not to obnoxiously bombard with questions or buy requests. Make sure to schedule it during your Planning Sundays, so you can focus on your book and maintenance social media the rest of the week.

If you're ready to kick it up or you feel like your growth is too slow, then learn everything you can about ads. I recommend starting with Facebook ads, because Facebook has the best interest data on the internet, aside from Google. The amount of stuff they know about us is scary, but extremely useful for marketing.

While ads are a whole separate book, one strategy is to pay $1 a day and let the page grow over time as the ad pushes readers to your email list or Amazon page. With the world becoming pay-to-play, if you want to grow your Facebook Page or sell books in Amazon, you'll have to buy ads. Amazon is the largest book retailer, and it's just become inevitable to learn how to create effective ads with them.

So that's it. That's a career's worth of advice on social media for authors. I hope it helps you get started or, if you're already started, get focused. As a writer, I completely understand how frustrating platform building and social media can be. I also understand the conflicting guidance, and I hope my method gives you a little less anxiety. It should be fun, and it should be efficient. We all want more time to write books.

If you'd like to discuss this further, ask questions or join the discussion, head on over to www.Facebook.com/Groups/ForAut horsBookSeries. The join question for the group is, "Where did Jenny first learn to surf?" The answer is: Barbados. (Hubs taught me on our honeymoon.)

In the words of the great New York Yankees' catcher Yogi Berra, "If you don't know where you're going, you'll end up someplace else." Let's make sure the place you end up is the place that gives you more time to write, grows your following, and helps you feel less overwhelmed. The writing life is so much fun, and I hope even the not-so-fun parts allow you to have a long and rewarding career.

If you have questions at all, please feel free to reach out to me at any time. You know by now; I want to hear from you!

Bonus Material

Bonus Material #1: Social Media Planning Guide and Tracker

Use this as a guide to planning out your author platform.

- I am creating an author platform for this reason (to be a *New York Times* bestseller, to build a following online, to grow an email distro list).
- My reader is ____ (define the reader – gender, age, occupation, hobbies).
- I will share ____ with my followers (define your public persona—pick 3 to 5 things you want to be known for).
- My social media posts will exist for this objective *(entertain, inform, or educate*).
- I will focus on these social media outlets. Pick one to three.
- I will focus on this type of content. Pick one to four.
- By this date, I will gain _____ (number) followers/emails.
- I will publish _____ many times a day on—
  - ☐ Facebook—no more than three.
  - ☐ YouTube—once a day or more.
  - ☐ Instagram—no more than once a day.
  - ☐ Twitter—four or more times a day.
  - ☐ Pinterest—at least once a day.
- My budget for marketing is ______.
- I will spend no more than ____ ($50)/month on ads while I'm testing ads.

- My Platform Planning day will be ___ (at least once a month).
    - □ I will schedule ___ posts on these social media outlets.
    - □ My social media content will include ____ (focus or content area).
- I will use ___ scheduler to schedule out my posts.
- My reader email will go out at this time every month.
- My reader email will include ______ (brainstorm a list of information ideas for your email).
- This day of the month, I will analyze the data on my social media and email, and brainstorm adjustments to my efforts (make a list).

Social Media Tracker

The tracker helps you plan out your content and track how well it's doing. Fill this out before scheduling the posts on a calendar or digital scheduler like Buffer or Hootsuite.

KEY: Social Media Outlet: FB-Facebook; YT-YouTube; IG-Instagram; T-Twitter; PT-Pinterest; **Content Type:** V-Video; A-Audio; G-Visual; H-Hodgepodge **Results**: L-Likes; C-Comments; S-Shares; I-Impressions

Date	SM Outlet	Content Type	Topic	Results: Likes, Comments, Shares, Impressions

Bonus Material #2: 162 Ideas for Digital Content Posts

This section compiles the list from the other sections of the book plus new ideas and offers a total of 162 ideas—enough ideas to incorporate over a year. Tips: Post one to three times a day on your Facebook Page; once a day on Instagram; videos shorter than four minutes on YouTube; as many photos as you need to on Pinterest boards; as many times as you want on Twitter but switch up the headlines for repeated web posts.

Poll FOLLOWERS about your Book/Business Needs

- Which book cover do you like?
- Which color is my main character's favorite?
- Which name do you like for a main character who is a funny, charismatic terrorist?
- What should I name my main character's dog/cat/parrot/iguana?
- How do you like to read? Print, ebook, audiobook?
- If you could meet one of my characters, which one and why?
- Where do you get your books: Amazon, library, or bookstore?
- I'm starting a YouTube channel/ podcast/blog. What would you like to know?
- Should I attend ______ (conference, workshop, retreat)?
- Which name is best for my main character/nemesis?
- Which author photo do you like best?
- Location data: who's been to Ireland? Is it true they only drink Guinness and tell bad jokes?

- Polls with yes/no or this/that questions.
- Polls with pics for a decision: Would my main character eat spaghetti or lasagna; visit Italy or Bali; spend her time in the library or sleeping off a hangover?
- Polls about what you should do: watch *Game of Thrones* or *The Marvelous Mrs. Maisel*; eat chocolate mousse or cheesecake from the menu at your dinner spot.
- Ask for recommendations when you're in a new location: things to do in Detroit or Branson.
- Any question related to your profession or expertise. Give two choices.

Fill in the blank

- If I had a million dollars, I would ______.
- If I were stuck on a desert island, I want ______ with me.
- On an airplane, I always take ______.
- My favorite food is ______.
- My favorite movie is ______.
- My favorite book is ______.
- The movie star most likely to play me in a movie is ______.
- ______ and ______ are necessities when taking a cruise/a hike/a trip.
- My favorite city on the planet is _____. Why?
- When you were ten, ____ was your favorite thing to do. (Post a pic)
- In 2010, I was living in ______.
- In 2020, I want to live in ______.

- If I could star in any show, it would be _____.
- I can't sleep because _____.
- If _____happened on my wedding day, then I would _____.
- Dear Lord, look at the size of that _____.
- Look out behind you, it's a _____.
- You're stronger than a _____.
- At the end of the rainbow is a _____.
- I work best when _____.
- Today I learned how to _____.
- The world is going to ____.
- Why does everyone have to be so _____?
- We can dance until we _____.
- Girls just wanna have _____.
- Once upon a time, _____ came over to my house.
- Best sport of all time is _____.
- Best athlete of all time is ____.
- Don't trust _____.
- I can't believe she stole my _____.
- I'm about to be arrested for _____.
- Where oh where is _____.
- If ____ would stop ____, he would _____.
- Shut up and _____.
- _____is a lie, there is only _____.

Ask questions

- Headed to ____(city)____. What do I bring?
- I need ______. Recommendations?
- I'm going to ______. Recommendations?
- Thoughts on latest movie.
- Thoughts on favorite book.
- What are you reading right now?
- What are you listening to right now?
- How do you spend your commute?
- How long is your commute?
- Favorite pastime while driving/flying?
- What's for lunch/dinner?
- Any questions about the subject matter you're writing that can evoke a debate or discussion.

Post your answer as GIFs

- How do you feel about ____ movie?
- How do you feel when eating Mexican food?
- How do you feel on the first day of school/on a Monday?
- How's your week going?
- Your reaction to the Oscars/Golden Globes/NCAA Final Four/Super Bowl.
- Describe your day with a GIF.
- Describe your understanding of (career field or field of study) with a GIF.

Share tips

- Baking/cooking tips.
- Alexa can _____.
- Best way to watch _____.
- Best biking gear is _____.
- Best place to hike is _____.
- Best fireworks spot.
- Best way to pick a lock.
- Best way to eavesdrop on _____.
- Quickest way to order delivery.
- Quickest route to _____.
- Best way to _____ (field of study).
- Fastest way to ____ (field of study).

Debates (ask for opinions or post a pic)

- Marvel or DC.
- Coke or Pepsi.
- Riverdale or Teen Wolf.
- Beach or Mountains.
- Football or Basketball.
- Sports or Gaming.
- Paris or Rome.
- Asia or Europe.
- Books or Movies.

- Desktops or Laptops.
- Apple or Android.
- Jeans or Yoga Pants.
- Sweatshirt or Sweater.
- Carbon or Oxygen.
- Torts or Claims.
- Democrat or Republican.
- Marathon or Ultra.
- Crossfit or Orange Theory.
- Weights or Cardio.
- Keto or Vegan.
- Netflix or Hulu.

Host a Contest or Giveaway

- Take a pic with my book and win free Kindle/gift card/dinner.
- Sign up for my newsletter and win tickets to movies/theater/ball game (relate it to your book if you can).
- Help me figure out a name for my main character and I'll use your name as a secondary character.
- Caption this photo to win a free book.
- Vote on which book I should put on sale.
- Refer five friends to my email list and win a free book/free extra chapter/free podcast episode.
- Tell me your story and win ____ (tie the request into what happens in your story).

- Conduct a scavenger hunt in one of your books or settings.
- Hold a recipe contest from your book.
- Ask trivia questions.
- Design a hero/monster/pet.
- Design a valentine.
- Hold a best Irish saying contest.
- Prompt for a slogan contest.
- Hold an Independence Day photo contest.
- I Spy (in your book, similar to a scavenger hunt).
- Worst/best date contests.

Spotify Lists

- My Spotify list for writing crime scenes.
- My Spotify list for writing sex scenes.
- My Spotify list for writing emotional scenes.
- My Spotify list when I write.
- My main character's Spotify list.
- My Spotify list while working out.
- My Spotify list while brainstorming.

Surveys

- Conduct surveys (never more than five to seven questions).
- Survey readers' likes and dislikes.

- Survey readers' needs in your newsletter.
- Survey readers' thoughts on one of your books (especially if you're doing a series).
- Survey readers about logistics of reading (where, when, how much time do you have to read).

Other posts

- Blogs you like.
- Podcasts you're listening to.
- YouTube videos/channels relevant to your followers.
- Tag a Facebook Page or Group.
- Interview with a subject matter expert in your field.
- Reviews: books, movies, products.
- Epic failures (that you've had or someone else).
- Why-I-don't posts (Don't Use a Mac; Don't Write on a Laptop; Don't Attend Conferences).
- Best-of lists (best books in your field; best hacks for productivity; best tips for ___; best products for your _____).
- Things you learned from _____ (current movies, books, people, news).
- FAQs about you, your product, services, or books.
- How-to lists (use something in your field, genre, book).
- Ultimate guides to _____.
- Case studies.
- Caption this photo.

- Book launch (no "buy my books" posts).
- Other authors' announcements (but don't flood your page with these).
- Anything behind the scenes.
- Funny posts (but if you aren't funny, don't try to be).
- Popular culture posts and your take on it.
- Caption a photo.
- Start a series—if you like Snickers bars, then post pics of that bar everywhere doing anything.
- Live author chats—posts only or video.
- Birthday parties.
- Favorite author/actor quotes.
- Character interviews.
- Jokes.
- #1 fan interviews/shout-outs/freebies.
- Survival kits in your world.
- Guess the ____ (location or object).

Bonus Material #3: Hashtags

Note: A hashtag is a way to categorize content for easy searching. Twitter users typically use fewer than three hashtags. Instagram is wide open, so use as many as 30, but use them in the comments, not the original post. Genre hashtags are popular for fiction; however, nonfiction hashtags outside of just a few have not broken out on these outlets yet. I recommend sticking with #Nonfiction and double-check the usage of your nonfiction category before using it as a hashtag.

Genre

#Autobiography

#Biography

#Business

#CEO

#Christian

#CivilWarHistory

#CozyMystery

#Documentary

#Entrepreneur

#Erotica

#Fantasy

#History

#Leadership

#Memoir

#Mystery

#Nonfiction

#Paranormal

#Poetry

#Romance

#RomanticSuspense

#Thriller

#TrueCrime

#SpyThriller

#UrbanFantasy

#WomensFiction

#YA (Young Adult)

Books and Reading

#AmReading

#Bibliophile

#BookBlogger

#Bookish

#BookLover

#BookNerd

#BookReview

#Books

#Bookshelf

#Bookstagrammer

#BookWorm

#Fiction

#FridayReads

#GreatReads

#IgReads

#IndieThursday

#Instabook

#Library

#LoveBooks

#MustRead

#NonfictionBooks

#Read

#Reading

#ReadersofInstagram

#WhatToRead

Promo

#99c

#AuthorRT

#BookGiveaway

#BookMarketing

#Deal

#FollowFriday

#FreeReads

#FreeBook

#FridayReads

#Novelines

#TeaserTues

Publishing/Self-Publishing

#Allie

#Amazon

#AskAgent

#AskAuthor

#AskEditor

#BookBuzz

#BookMarketing

#D2D (Draft 2 Digital)

#EBook

#Ebooks

#Entrepreneur

#GetPublished

#ePubChat

#eReaders

#IndieAuthors

#iPad

#Kindle

#KindleBargain

#Kobo

#KDP (Kindle Direct Publishing)

#MSWL (manuscript wishlist, where agents and editors post what they are looking for)

#Nook

#Publishing

#Review

#SelfPub

#SmashWords

Writing Process or Community

#1K1H (1,000 words an hour challenge)

#AmWriting

#AmEditing

#CopyWriting

#Creativity

#Editing

#IndieAuthor

#KidLit

#KidLitChat

#NaNoWriMo (National Novel Writing Month)

#MysteryWriter

#NonfictionWriter

#NonfictionWriting

#Poetry

#RomanceWriter

#SciFiChat

#StoryStarter

#ThrillerWriter

#WIP (Work in Progress)

#WordAThon

#WordCount

#WriteChat

#WriteGoal

#WriteMotivation

- #WriteTip
- #WriterWednesday
- #WritersLife
- #Writing
- #WritingBlitz
- #WritingCommunity
- #WritingPrompt
- #WriterCommunity
- #WritersCommunity
- #WritersofIg
- #WritersofInstagram
- #WritersofTwitter
- #YALit
- #YoungAdult

Bonus Material #4: Annual Holidays Calendar

JANUARY

1	New Year's Day
1	National Bloody Mary Day
2	National Science Fiction Day
2	National Creampuff Day
3	National Chocolate Covered Cherry Day
4	World Braille Day
4	Trivia Day
5	National Whipped Cream Day
6	Epiphany
8	Clean off your desk day
11	National Human Trafficking Awareness Day
12	National Youth Day
14	Organize your home Day
15	Robert E Lee's Birthday
15	Idaho Human Rights Day
15	National Wikipedia Day
15	Civil Rights Day
18	Thesaurus Day
21	National Hugging Day
22	Hotsauce Day
23	National Pie Day
23	Handwriting Day
24	National Peanut Butter Day
25	Opposite Day
25	Robert Burns Day/Night
27	National Family Literacy Day
27	National Chocolate Cake Day

29	Kansas Day
31	Tu Bishvat Jewish Holiday
31	National Gorilla Suit Day
2nd Monday	Martin Luther King Jr Day

FEBRUARY

1	National Freedom Day
2	Groundhog Day
2	National Wear Red Day
2	National Tater Tot Day
4	Rosa Parks Day
9	National Pizza Day & National Bagel Day
10	Umbrella Day
11	Make a Friend Day
12	Darwin Day
13	Maha Shivaratri (Hindu Holiday)
13	World Radio Day
14	Valentine's Day
15	Susan B Anthony's Birthday
15	World Earthworm Day
16	Elizabth Peratrovich Day in Alaska
17	Random Acts of Kindness Day
19	Daisy Gatson Bates Day in Arkansas
22	National Margarita Day
22	World Thinking Day
23	National Banana Bread Day
26	Tell a Fairy Tale Day
28	Linus Pauling Day in Oregon
1st Saturday	Ice Cream for Breakfast Day
1st Sunday	Super Bowl Sunday
2nd Monday	Lincoln's Birthday
2nd Tuesday	Mardi Gras
2nd Tuesday	National Frozen Yogurt Day

2nd Wednesday	Ash Wednesday
2nd Friday	Chinese New Year
3rd Monday	President's Day

MARCH

1	Purim (Jewish Holiday)
1	St David's Day
1	National Peanut Butter Lover's Day
2	Holi (Hindu Holiday)
2	Read Across America Day
2	Dr Seuss Birthday
2	Employee Appreciation Day
3	World Wildlife Day
7	Alexander Graham Bell Day (Do you remember your childhood phone #)
8	International Women's Day
13	Jewel Day
14	Pi Day
17	World Sleep Day
17	St Patrick's Day
18	Awkward Moment's Day
20	Spring Equinox
20	International Day of Happiness
21	World Poetry Day
21	World Puppetry Day
22	National Corndog Day
22	International Goof Off Day
26	Prince Jonah Kuhio Kalanianaole Day in Hawaii
26	Sewards Day in Alaska
27	International Whiskey Day
29	National Vietnam War Veterans Day

30	Take a Walk in a Park Day
SPRING	Jewish Passover, Christian Good Friday, Holy Thursday & Easter occur approximately six weeks after Mardi Gras but the exact date differs every year; Passover ends approximately a week after it begins
2nd Sunday	Daylight Savings Time starts
4th Sunday	Palm Sunday

APRIL

1	April Fool's Day
2	National Peanut Butter and Jelly Day
2	International Children's Book Day
2	Pascua Florida Day in Florida
4	Tell a Lie Day
5	National Caramel Day & National Burrito Day
6	Maryland Day in Maryland
6	National Tartan Day
7	National Beer Day
7	Day of Remembrance for Victims of Rwandan Genocide
10	National Cinnamon Roll Day
10	National Library Worker's Day
10	Siblings Day
12	National Grilled Cheese Sandwich Day
13	Thomas Jefferson's Birthday
15	Father Damien Day in Hawaii
16	Wear Pajamas to Work Day
17	National Cheeseball Day
17	Haiku Day
17	Tax Day

19	Bicycle Day
21	National Tea Day
22	Oklahoma Day in Oklahoma
22	National Jellybean Day
22	Earth Day
22	World Book and Copyright Day
24	National Pigs in a Blanket Day
25	National Zucchini Bread Day
25	Administrative Professionals Day
26	Take our Sons and Daughters to Work Day
26	National Pretzel Day & Poem in Your Pocket Day
29	International Dance Day
30	International Jazz Day
30	National Honesty Day
3rd Thursday	National High Five Day

MAY

1	Law Day
3	National Day of Prayer
3	World Press Freedom Day
4	International Firefighters Day
4	Stars Wars Day
5	Cinco de Mayo
5	International Midwives Day
6	National Nurse's Day
6	International No Diet Day
8	Truman Day in Missouri
11	National Eat What You Want Day
11	Military Spouse Appreciation Day
12	Limerick Day
15	Peace Officers Memorial Day
16	National BBQ Day

17	National Walnut Day
18	International Museum Day
19	Armed Forces Day
20	World Metrology Day
20	World Bee Day
21	Talk Like Yoda Day
22	National Maritime Day
22	Harvey Milk Day in California
23	National Taffy Day
23	World Turtle Day
25	Towel Day – tribute to the late Douglas Adams
25	National Wine Day
25	Geek Pride Day
25	National Missing Children's Day
26	National Paper Airplane Day
28	National Burger Day
1st Week	National Postcard Week
1st Friday	No Pants Day
1st Saturday	Kentucky Derby
1st Sunday	World Laughter Day
2nd Saturday	Preakness Stakes
2nd Sunday	Mother's Day
3rd Friday	National Pizza Party Day
3rd Sunday	Pentecost
4th Sunday	Memorial Day

JUNE

1	Say Something Nice Day
2	National Rocky Road Day
3	National Chocolate Macaron Day
3	World Bicycle Day
4	National Cheese Day

5	National Gingerbread Day & National Moonshine Day
6	D-Day
7	Chocolate Ice Cream Day
8	World Ocean's Day
10	National Iced Tea Day
11	National Corn on the Cob Day & National German Chocolate Cake Day
12	Anne Frank Day
14	U.S. Army Birthday
14	World Blood Donor Day
14	Flag Day
16	World Juggling Day
17	Bunker Hill Day
17	National Eat Your Vegetables Day
20	National Vanilla Milkshake Day
20	American Eagle Day
20	International Surfing Day
21	Summer Solstice
21	Go Skateboarding Day
21	International Yoga Day
21	World Music Day
23	Typewriter Day
24	Take Your Dog to Work Day
25	National Catfish Day
26	National Chocolate Pudding Day
28	National Ceviche Day & National Tapioca Day
28	CAPS LOCK DAY
1st Friday	National Donut Day
1st Sunday	National Cancer Survivors Day
2nd Saturday	Belmont Stakes
2nd Sunday	Father's Day

JULY

1	National Gingersnap Day
2	World UFO Day
3	Eat Beans Day
4	Independence Day
4	National Caesar Salad Day & National BBQ Day
5	National Apple Turnover Day
6	National Fried Chicken Day
6	World Kissing Day
7	Macaroni Day
7	World Chocolate Day
10	National Pina Colada Day
11	National Blueberry Muffin Day
11	Cheer Up the Lonely Day
12	National Pecan Pie Day
13	National French Fries Day
13	Embrace your Geekness Day
14	Bastille Day
15	Gummi Worm Day
15	World Youth Skills Day
16	Spinach Day
17	World Emoji Day
18	Nelson Mandela International Day
19	Stick Out Your Tongue Day
20	National Fortune Cookie Day
23	National Hot Dog Day
24	National Drive Thru Day & National Tequila Day
24	Cousins Day
25	National Hot Fudge Sundae Day
25	Christmas in July
27	National Korean War Veterans Armistice

	Day
29	National Lasagna Day & National Chicken Wing Day
30	National Cheesecake Day
30	International Day of Friendship
31	Uncommon Musical Instrument Day
1st Saturday	International Free Hugs Day
3rd Sunday	Parents Day
3rd Sunday	National Ice Cream Day
4th Thursday	National Chili Dog Day

AUGUST

1	Colorado Day in Colorado
3	National Watermelon Day
4	U.S. Coast Guard Birthday
5	Sisters Day
6	National Root Beer Float Day
7	Purple Heart Day
7	Lighthouse Day
9	Book Lovers Day
10	National Smores Day
12	International Youth Day
13	International Lefthanders Day
14	National Creamsicle Day
15	National Lemon Meringue Pie Day
17	Thrift Shop Day
19	National Potato Day
19	National Aviation Day
20	World Mosquito Day
21	World Senior Citizens Day
21	Senior Citizens Day
22	National Eat a Peach Day
24	National Peach Pie Day & National Waffle

	Day
25	National Banana Split Day
26	Women's Equality Day
27	Lyndon Baines Johnson Day in Texas
27	National Banana Lovers Day
27	World Rock-Paper-Scissors Day
29	National Sports Day
31	Eat Outside Day
1st Wednesday	Professional Engineers Day
1st Friday	International Beer Day
1st Saturday	National Mustard Day
2nd Wednesday	Assumption of Mary
Mid-Month	Eid al-Adha (Muslim Holiday)
3rd Saturday	National Honey Bee Day

SEPTEMBER

1	Random Acts of Kindness Day
3	Skyscraper Day
4	National Macadamia Nut Day
5	International Day of Charity
5	Be Late for Something Day
6	Read a Book Day
7	National Acorn Squash Day
8	International Literacy Day
8	World Physical Therapy Day
9	National Grandparents Day
11	Patriot Day
13	International Chocolate Day (Birthday of Milton S. Hershey
13	Positive Thinking Day (PMA)
14	Hug Your Hound Day
15	National Cleanup Day
16	National Guacamole Day

16	National Cinnamon Raisin Bread Day
17	National Apple Dumpling Day
17	Constitution and Citizenship Day
18	U.S. Air Force Birthday
19	International Talk Like a Pirate Day
20	National Pepperoni Pizza Day
21	International Day of Peace (United Nations)
21	National POW/MIA Recognition Day
22	Autumn Equinox
22	Hobbit Day
26	Johnny Appleseed Day
26	National Pancake Day & National Dumpling Day
26	Love Note Day
27	Crush a Can Day
27	World Tourism Day
28	Eat Dinner with Your Children Day
28	Native American's Day in California
28	Ask a Stupid Question Day
29	National Coffee Day
30	Gold Star Mother's Day
1st Monday	Labor Day
Early Month	Rosh Hashana (Jewish Holiday)
Mid-Month	Yom Kippur (Jewish Holiday)

OCTOBER

1	Child Health Day
1	World Vegetarian Day
4	Feast of St Francis of Assisi (Christian Holiday)
4	National Taco Day
5	World Teacher's Day

6	National Noodle Day
6	Britain's National Poetry Day
9	Leif Erikson Day
13	U.S. Navy Birthday
14	National Dessert Day
15	I Love Lucy Day
16	Boss's Day
17	National Pasta Day
17	Wear Something Gaudy Day
18	Alaska Day in Alaska
18	National Chocolate Cupcake Day
20	International Observe the Moon Night
21	International Day of the Nacho
22	National Nut Day
26	Nevada Day in Nevada
27	Author's Day
28	National Chocolate Day
29	National Oatmeal Day
29	National Cat Day
31	Halloween / All Hallow's Eve / All Hallow's Read
1st Friday	World Smile Day
2nd Monday	Columbus Day

NOVEMBER

1	All Saint's Day (Christian Holiday)
1	World Vegan Day
2	All Soul's Day (Christian Holiday)
3	National Sandwich Day
6	National Nachos Day
10	U.S. Marine Corps Birthday
11	Veteran's Day / Armistice Day ending WWI
12	National Chicken Soup for the Soul Day

12	National Happy Hour Day
13	World Kindness Day
14	National Pickle Day
15	Day of the Imprisoned Writer
15	National Clean Out Your Refrigerator Day
17	National Homemade Bread Day
19	World Toilet Day (UN designated)
20	National Absurdity Day
21	World Hello Day
21	National Stuffing Day
23	National Cashew Day
26	National Cake Day
1st Sunday	Daylight Savings Time Ends
1st Sunday	New York City Marathon
1st Wednesday	National Eating Healthy Day
1st Thursday	National Men Make Dinner Day
1st Friday	Love Your Lawyer Day
2nd Tuesday	Election Day
3rd Thursday	Thanksgiving
3rd Thursday	World Philosophy Day
3rd Friday	Black Friday
4th Monday	Cyber Monday

DECEMBER

1	Eat a Red Apple Day
4	National Cookie Day
6	St Nicholas Day
6	Put on Your Shoes Day
7	Pearl Harbor Remembrance Day
7	Letter Writing Day
11	National Have a Bagel Day
11	International Mountain Day
12	Feast of Our Lady of Guadalupe

13	U.S. National Guard Birthday
13	National Hot Cocoa Day
14	Monkey Day
15	National Cupcake Day
17	Pan American Aviation Day
17	Wright Brothers Day
17	National Maple Syrup Day
20	National Sangria Day
21	Winter Solstice
21	Ugly Sweater Day
23	Festivus Day
24	Christmas Eve
25	Christmas
25	National Pumpkin Pie Day
31	New Year's Eve
31	Make Up Your Mind Day
1st Sunday	First Sunday of Advent (Christian Holiday)
1st Monday	First Day of Hanukkah (Jewish Holiday) – ends after ten days
2nd Saturday	Feast of the Immaculate Conception (Christian Holiday)

Acknowledgments

No book comes into the world without a tribe of people to get it there. I want to thank Pikes Peak Writers, Washington Romance Writers, all members of the Writer Nation Facebook Group, and every writer I've ever met for being my tribe.

Years ago, I stumbled onto a conference in Colorado Springs and found a group of people so supportive of each other that I knew I needed to be a part of it. I can't thank them enough for supporting me, even if they didn't know they were: Susan Mitchell, Deb Courtney, Sharon Manislovich, Rebecca Davis, Jason Henry, MK Meredith, Kameron Claire, Laura Hayden, Mandy Houke, Chris Mandeville, Brinn Colenda, Jax Bubis, Becky Clark, Erin Kohler, Kim Lajevardi, Mardra Sikora, Shannon Lawrence, Deidre

Greenly, JT Evans, Kathie Scrimgeour, Ed Raetz, Laura Chambers, Aaron Michael Ritchey, Dawn Smit Miller, Julie Kazimer, Todd Fahnestock, Jem Welch, Barbara Nickless, Jennie Marts, David Slayton, Nick Hight, Cindi Madsen, Jessica McDonald, Jade Farrar, Cameron Eickenmeyer, Kristi Lloyd, Antonio Salinas, Robert Spiller, Pam McCutcheon, Aaron Brown, Kevin Ikenberry, Mario Acevedo, Warren Hammond, and Angie Hodapp.

After we moved to Washington, DC, I found yet another wonderful group of supportive writers: Jessica Snyder, Keely Thrall, Lori Ann Bailey, Kelly Maher, Jean Marie Ward, Diana Cosby, Deborah Barnhart, Angele McQuade, Kathy Seidel, Jamie Farrell, Julie Halperson, Andie J. Christopher, Harper Kincaid, Michele Sandiford, Gigi Gabriel, Miguelina Perez, Misha Crews, Meredith Bond, Mindy Klasky, Cara Allen, JT Bock, Robin Covington, Yvonne Pinney, Kerri Carpenter, James Burns, and Tiffany Yates Martin.

Other groups include the Music City Romance Writers, Mystery Writers of America mid-Atlantic chapter, and the Bay-to-Oceans Writers plus AJ Scudiere, Liz Caraway, Isaac Cubillos, Helena Kaufman, and so many others.

Abigail Riccardi, my virtual assistant and sanity check. Sandra Wendel, my amazing editor who knows how to tell me when my stuff sucks and when it doesn't. Mark and Lorna Reid for exceptional insight into the industry. Lexie Rayburn for helping me focus the brand.

Brad Kimberly for helping me with my wreck of a website. Chris Watt for years of graphics help, since I'm hopeless in that area.

I can't close this book without thanking my family, and especially my husband, Travis Herbranson, for having an unshakable belief that I could write and actually finish this book and many others.

Thank you, honey, for giving me the strength and wings to chase a dream a long time coming.

I hope I haven't forgotten anyone, but rest assured if you've passed through my writing life, you've made an impression, and I can't thank you enough.

About the Author

Jennifer Lovett Herbranson has been a communicator, marketer, teacher, and public relations professional since 2001. She has party planned for the US Ambassador to Portugal, managed location production for Hollywood filmmakers, and eaten lunch with a famous late-night television host (it was Taco Bell). She has provided speech input to the President of the United States and the Secretary of Energy, has been quoted by the *New York Times, CNN, FoxNews,* and *Time*, and provided research opportunities for writers, professors, documentary filmmakers, and members of Congress. With her husband, she co-founded Writer Nation, an online community for writers providing essential marketing tips and advice for building an author platform and for finding more readers.

Jenny Kate—as her friends call her—issues the monthly *Writer Nation Report*, a publishing and marketing industry newsletter with tips, advice, news, and information, and *The Blitz*, a monthly shorter burst of industry news meant to inspire authors to finish their work. She is also the host of the *Writer Nation Podcast* where she chats with writers and industry professionals in all stages of their careers.

She holds a master's degree in English from Tennessee State University and a master's degree in international relations from the University of Oklahoma. She blogs for Pikes Peak Writers, judges contests for the Utah League of Writers, and is the communications director for Washington Romance Writers.

A born Alabama girl, she bleeds crimson and white. When she isn't writing or teaching about marketing, she travels the world looking for the world's best vegan sandwich. So far, tofu banh mi in Hoi An, Vietnam, is winning that race.

She lives in Northern Virginia with her husband and daughter.

Feel free to reach out to her anytime with marketing or publishing questions:

Web: www.thewriternation.com

Twitter: @writernationjen

Instagram: @writernationjen

Facebook.com/WriterNation

Facebook.com/groups/ForAuthorsBookSeries *(challenge question answer is Barbados)*

Email: writernationjen@gmail.com

Printed in Great Britain
by Amazon

70079676R00108